MAKE IT RAIN!

MAKE IT RAIN!

How to Use the Media to Revolutionize Your Business & Brand

AREVA MARTIN, ESQ
With DONNA BEECH

CENTER
STREET

NEW YORK   NASHVILLE

Center Street
Hachette Book Group
1290 Avenue of the Americas, New York, NY 10104
centerstreet.com
twitter.com/centerstreet

First Edition: March 2018

Center Street is a division of Hachette Book Group, Inc. The Center Street name and logo are trademarks of Hachette Book Group, Inc.

The publisher is not responsible for websites (or their content) that are not owned by the publisher.

The Hachette Speakers Bureau provides a wide range of authors for speaking events. To find out more, go to www.HachetteSpeakersBureau.com or call (866) 376-6591.

Library of Congress Cataloging-in-Publication Data has been applied for.

ISBNs: 978-1-4789-8987-5 (hardcover), 978-1-4789-8986-8 (ebook)

Printed in the United States of America

LSC-C

10 9 8 7 6 5 4 3 2

To Ernest, Michael, Morgan, and Marty
You inspire me...

Contents

PART IV
AMPLIFY IT!

PART V
MONETIZE IT

Foreword by Dr. Phil McGraw

There is no substitute for talent, but it is not enough. To be successful on the national broadcast stage takes some luck. And the harder you work, the "luckier" you get.

Areva Martin has that rare combination of unprecedented talent, "in the trenches" experience, and a passionate, driven work ethic that makes her impossible to exclude from any relevant narrative.

In *Make It Rain!*, she provides invaluable advice about how to leverage the incredible power of the media to get your message out to the people who need it most. She shares the inner workings of the fast-moving, sophisticated world of "experting" on the national broadcast stage. I should know: I have the No. 1 syndicated informational talk show on TV, and Areva Martin is my No. 1 expert. She always delivers.

It's tough out there. Inside information can let you know how to present your expertise to bookers and producers in the most effective ways and give you an edge that helps you stand out from the competition.

I've always believed that, if you hope to succeed, you need to build a strong core of supporters who share your visions and your passions. It's a proven way to make important things happen.

That's exactly what Areva Martin's dynamic new book, *Make It Rain!*, is all about. With her own expertise at using social media to leverage her TV appearances into a platform that continues to grow at astounding rates, she shows you how to break into radio, podcasts, cable, and national TV. This book will help you get out of your comfort zone—the ways of building your business and your brand that have taken you only so far. It can be frightening, but if you want things to change, you've got to take action. *Make It Rain!* will show you how to make those efforts succeed.

Areva is the first true expert to reveal these secrets about how TV news works behind the scenes. This is how the pros do it. Anyone hoping to become a thought leader in today's competitive market will find this book invaluable. One chapter alone, "Jump on Breaking News Stories," is worth the price of the book.

I believe in a "defined product." Areva tells you exactly how to define yourself as an expert and "own your lane" to become the go-to resource when your subject is pushed front and center in the country's collective consciousness.

Areva Martin made her first TV appearance as an expert on my show. It was immediately obvious that she had a lot to offer. When I asked for her opinion, she answered with powerful, poignant statements that went right to the heart of the issue. Her insights always help clarify the pivotal issues. And with all her energy and panache, the camera loves her.

Areva is now a part of the *Dr. Phil* family, regularly appearing on my show and co-hosting one of the other Stage 29 productions, the Emmy Award-winning daytime show *The Doctors*.

I'm delighted that she has written this book to share the skills she demonstrates every time she's on the air. On my show, I can always rely on the fact that Areva never strays from the goal of the show; she follows my lead, treats the guests with respect, doesn't compete for the mic, and always comes prepared. These are exactly the qualities every show is looking for.

Make It Rain! will be a great tool for all of my producers as they prepare experts for appearances on *Dr. Phil*. Following Areva's well-articulated guidelines and watching her appearances is the formula for assured success.

Well done, Areva!

Introduction:
The Call That
Changed My Life

Making media appearances is one of the best things I've ever done. When I learned how to amplify those opportunities on multiple levels—using the techniques I'm going to show you in this book—it utterly revolutionized my business and made me a rainmaker. To this day, it's still one of the best tools I've got.

Stepping up and into the limelight gives me the honor of taking part in some of the most important conversations happening around the world today. It lets me reach more people than ever before on the issues I'm most passionate about. Whether it's a shooting in a high school, the unfair treatment of a special needs child, or a question of civil rights, I'm asked to shed light on complex social and legal issues five to seven days a week on shows like *Good Morning America*, *CNN Tonight*, *Anderson Cooper 360°*, *CNN International*, *The Doctors*, and *Dr. Phil*.

I was always taught that when you're lucky enough to learn something or have some advantage, you should share it. When you do, it will come back to you a thousandfold. So this is my chance to share with you a great opportunity and your chance to step into the limelight and share with others the knowledge and experience that you've worked so hard to develop all these years.

If you're like me, you had no childhood dreams of being an expert on TV. Growing up in a housing projects in North St.

Louis, I was about as far from Hollywood as you can imagine. My fondest dream was to work hard enough to get into law school so I could make a real difference in people's lives.

With years of loving help from my mother, grandmother, and her best friend, my godmother, I realized that dream. After graduating from Harvard Law, I opened a practice that grew to be one of the largest female-owned, African-American law firms in LA. I was a typical trial attorney: working twelve- and fourteen-hour days, arguing cases in court, asking questions in depositions, and toiling away on complicated legal briefs into the night.

One day I was contacted by the parents of five nonverbal autistic kids in Las Vegas. They were beyond upset. A teacher had been abusing their kids. The evidence was so clear and so appalling that we decided to sue. Because it was one of the first times a teacher had been prosecuted in Las Vegas for child abuse in a school setting, it made headlines.

That was when I got a call from the *Dr. Phil* show.

The producers told me they had seen the story and wanted to invite my clients on the show to talk about child abuse in schools and kids with autism. They knew their audience would be interested in hearing what parents ought to look for and how they should respond in similar situations.

As their lawyer, I was invited to be on the show with them. Although I later became a legal expert on the show, that first day, I was there to give my clients moral support and advance the story by explaining what was going on with the criminal case and the civil lawsuit we had filed.

When the show aired, I was shocked to see how many calls I received. It took two days to return them all.

Parents across the country had seen the show and wanted to hire my firm to handle problems they were having related to their kids and school districts and other organizations. Some were the parents of special needs kids; others were not. Many of them said they'd been worried about similar situations at school or elsewhere, but simply hadn't known whom to call! After seeing me on TV, they felt like they could trust me with their story and they knew I would help.

My staff and I had to scramble to handle all the new referrals. It was a great windfall. But apart from that, I started to think about how much I enjoyed being on the show. For one thing, the staff on the *Dr. Phil* show had been wonderful. Their high level of professionalism and commitment to making the show great was an inspiration. And I couldn't shake that moment when the lights went up, the cameras turned to face us, and a wave of excitement rustled through the audience. We were taping a show that would be transformative for families across the country! Millions of people would watch and listen to every word we said.

No moment has given me a stronger urge than that one to be at my very best. To come away from that, knowing you've risen to the occasion and given it all you've got, feels good. It was a defining experience for me. I wanted to do more.

While I was on the set, the producers had asked if I had other specialties as an expert. It gave me a chance to fill them in briefly on my background and let them know about other kinds of stories where I could provide valuable information. Producers of talk shows have to come up with memorable new episodes every day of the week. They were happy to give me their contact information and invite me to call them if any other cases of interest came up. It made me start looking at talk and news shows in a completely new way, and after taking them up on their offer, I was appearing regularly on *Dr. Phil*, which led to appearances on other shows.

Every night for years I'd watched TV interviews with legal experts and assumed they had connections that I would never have. Not until I started going on these shows myself did I discover that most of the time, the only difference between experts being interviewed on TV and those sitting at home watching was that the ones on TV had defined their brand, identified an audience, and took the first critical step of pitching a producer.

My goal in writing this book is to empower, inform, and educate you on how to use the media, as I have over the last ten years, to revolutionize your business, explode your sales, build your platform, and maybe even become one of America's most sought-after thought leaders—in short, I'm going to show you how to make it rain!

PART I

RAINMAKING

CHAPTER 1

Make Your Own Luck

I t's happening right in front of you every day. On network TV, broadcast radio, Internet radio, podcasts, blogs, and live streams, guest experts are getting local and national exposure for their businesses and brands that they could never have afforded to reach with ads.

The smart ones—the rainmakers—are amplifying every single appearance by magnitudes across a vast web of influencers to reach thousands or millions more on social media.

What if you could get this kind of movie star visibility for your brand? How would you like to get your business or organization in front of millions of prospects with the avid endorsement of the hosts—without spending a dime?

In *Make It Rain!* I'll show you exactly how to do it. It's not as easy as making a phone call to Lester Holt, the anchor on *Dateline NBC*, or Candi Carter, the executive producer of *The View*, and saying, "Hi, I'd like for you to feature me as an expert tonight!" But it's far less complicated and intimidating than you think. And the rewards are unbelievable.

With as little as a three-minute segment, an expert can persuade someone to vote for a candidate, shop at a local mall, move a government agency to change its policy, subscribe to a website, register for an event, or show up for a march. What's more, it can flood your business with new clients. The first time I came back to my office after making a media appearance as a guest expert, piles of messages from new prospects were waiting for me, and because I'd talked passionately about my brand message on the show, they were already well-qualified leads.

After almost a decade as a guest expert on everything from local podcasts to the top cable and network shows, I can tell you that as powerful as media appearances can be, they're not just for megastars. You can get in this game.

But, of course, there are a few caveats. You have to know how to match your brand to the right audience and venues, craft a pitch that producers can't resist, make sure you're 100 percent on message with your talking points, follow the Rule of 4, and amplify it all.

In the chapters ahead, I'll reveal what only insiders know about the power of media appearances to revolutionize your business. If you want to grow your revenue, increase your followers, raise awareness for your cause, or build a stellar personal brand, you need the skills and savvy to make it rain. By the time you finish this book, you'll know how.

Who Are the Experts?

You may not realize that a lot of the experts you see in the media are just like you. Most are not paid contributors. They don't work for the network or a particular show in any capacity. They aren't so famous that the executive producer from MSNBC has them on speed dial and calls them for every show.

The anchors, hosts, and reporters, and some contributors who we see on TV regularly are working for the networks and media channels. People like Anderson Cooper, Brian Williams, Kate Bolduan, Christiane Amanpour, and Shepard Smith are career newscasters. These top-echelon experts are in such high demand that they have made it a career. Signing an exclusive with a particular network, they command six- and seven-figure-plus contracts paid on retainer or by appearance.

But by far, most of the experts emerging today are not under contract. They are savvy businesspeople and influencers who have learned how to leverage media appearances to reach tens of thousands, or even millions, of new customers, to increase their authority and cache in their field, and to magnify their message in vitally important ways.

Most likely, none of the experts being interviewed on your favorite network and cable shows were paid to appear. They don't work for the station or the show. A savvy person with verifiable expertise approaches the producers of a show with a pitch, explaining their credentials and talking points. And if it fits with the story the show is covering, the expert is now sitting on a studio set sharing his or her expertise with millions with the tacit endorsement of the host, the show, and the network.

In today's 24/7 media, producers have to book so many guests, they have long since run through their own personal lists of experts. They rely on referrals or pitches from publicists, bookers, and the experts themselves to match the best person with the news of the hour.

This creates the perfect opportunity for business owners, professionals, authors, and experts of all kinds. Everyone from firefighters to sushi chefs who are experts in their fields can enter the mainstream conversation taking place on myriad media channels to voice their opinions and talk about their expertise. Although they are not paid by the networks, they can reap huge benefits. But only a fraction of qualified experts are taking advantage of these incredible opportunities. That's one reason why this is an ideal time for you to get involved.

Who Are the Rainmakers?

Tribal societies around the world have relied on rainmakers for centuries to magically bring back prosperity to the land in times of drought. Without enough water, the crops wilted, the livestock suffered, and the very survival of the tribe was cast in doubt.

In North America, Native American medicine men made it rain for settlers in exchange for trade. In China, mysterious Wu shamans danced in a ring of fire, until the rain came down like the drops of sweat on their brows. Farmers in Thailand ceremonially drenched their water-hating cats to bring on the rain. Young girls in Romania danced through the streets, singing songs of supplication to Dodola, the Slavic goddess of rain.

Today corporate rainmakers may not resort to a rain dance, but their methods are equally mysterious. A few words whispered in the right ears, a friendly game of golf, an invitation to an exclusive event—simple things, yet somehow the rainmaker knows how to wield them to produce the desired result, as if by magic. That's what rainmaking is.

In today's 24/7 media cycles, rainmakers are experts who are not only visible in the media, but who also leverage that media to build revenue, followers, and influence.

If you are only an expert, without leveraging all the media channels available to you, you're not a rainmaker. If you're a social media influencer with thousands of followers, but haven't figured out how to convert that into revenue, you're not a rainmaker. You need revenue, followers, and influence to create that magical synergy that is more than the sum of its parts, that results in influence, abundance, and power. Rainmakers don't sit around hoping for a lucky break. They take the initiative and make their own luck!

What Is the Payoff?

Making frequent appearances in the media brings in so many prospective new clients to my law firm that it's virtually eliminated our marketing budget. A single interview can generate more response than I could ever have gotten with paid advertising.

Most shows actually have many more viewers and reach a

much bigger audience on their websites and social media than they do on TV. Unlike a print display ad, any appearance you make can be amplified a thousandfold on social media. It can be used for your next pitch and as your calling card to connect with more producers.

Even a relatively small Fox affiliate in Cleveland, WJW-TV, reaches 1.1 million on social media. The local affiliate of MSNBC in Atlanta had over 33.6 million page views in 2015 alone.

The beauty is, TV viewers have already opted in. You're not forcing an ad into their line of sight. They're expecting to like what you have to say. Out of all the stations they could watch, they're watching this one. With so much competition, that's more of a vote of confidence than it's ever been before. And here you are, talking to the host they listen to regularly, about issues that are closely connected to your brand.

Can you imagine trying to get that same TV host to endorse your business or display ad? Not likely to ever happen. But if you appear as an expert on a show, for those three to five minutes on the air, the host is asking your opinion and listening to your advice. It immediately imbues you with validation, authority, and cache, as if by magic. Many entrepreneurs read books about social media marketing and analytics, they hire crews of people to manage their SEO, ROI, KPI—or whatever metrics are most popular at the time for getting their brand in front of their target market. They spend a fortune on advertising and promotion and giveaways. It's all part of building a platform and brand in a competitive environment. But despite all of this hard work to be seen by the right audience, they're missing the golden ring.

A single appearance on the right TV show would allow them to speak directly to their audience. Not only that, but media appearances give them what would be rare or nearly impossible with ordinary promotions: an implicit endorsement by the famous host that the viewer already likes enough to watch every day or week.

In 2017, Lu Kang of the Chinese Ministry of Foreign Affairs was interviewed by Richard Engel on NBC News about trade relations. Laverne Cox, an actress from *Orange Is the New Black*, talked with Chris Matthews about transgender rights on MSNBC's *Hardball*. Brian Kelley, the chief content officer for *U.S. News & World Report*, appeared on *CBS This Morning* to talk about the best states in the country with Gayle King. Each of the people being interviewed were experts who were most likely not paid to appear and did not work for the networks.

Media appearances can give you the opportunity to make your expertise available, to raise the profile of your business, and to get your message out. If you inform, educate, and empower people in the process, producers will be quick to invite you back. Those invitations can lead to a dramatic uptick in business.

When I asked my friend Eric Guster whether or not appearing as an expert on local TV has affected his bottom line, he told me flat out, "My revenue has quadrupled. Television gives name recognition and credibility. I get calls now from all over the country and leads on new cases. It's been great. A local television presence helped tremendously."

Dr. Jennifer Berman, who cohosts *The Doctors* with me and often provides medical commentary on network and cable shows, says that her appearances on TV provide a lot of calls and interest in her work, as well as a platform that she can leverage for greater opportunities and access to relationships with other brands. For Dr. Berman, the high visibility has also helped her to support nonprofits and other causes that she believes in.

Like Dr. Berman, media appearances have been incredibly important to my philanthropy. Later in the book, I'll talk about the incredible fund-raising opportunities it has made possible for my nonprofit, Special Needs Network. By raising your stature and profile, you can drive more donations, enlist more involvement, and maintain a much higher visibility for the causes that ignite your passion. Whether you have an expertise in a profession, like law, science, and medicine, or a special interest, like consumer reports, movie reviews, and cooking, there has never been a greater need for experts who are willing to step up and there have never been more people listening.

That said, media appearances are not advertising. You never say anything like:

"Yes, Matt, that tragic accident resulted from a broken axle that could've been fixed by a mechanic who knew what that vibration underneath the car meant. At Murphy's Car Parts, we'd never let that kind of thing happen. And in fact, we've got a sale on axles this week!"

A successful guest appearance requires a lot more finesse. You need to employ the skills discussed in this book. You'll learn how to weave your message into the talking points instead of pushing your own agenda, how to get the host to ask you questions that open the door to issues that matter most for the show's audience and your business, and how to pivot to your message when the conversation starts heading another way. As you practice the skills in the chapters that follow, they'll soon become second nature.

Over the years, I've met so many experts who appear regularly on TV. A few find they love it so much, they decide to make a career as an anchor, host, or paid analyst, but not all of them do. Some are invested in growing a business that offers a product or a service, or expanding a brand that is tied to a social or political cause. Whatever your message, there's no better way to get the word out than by appearing as an expert. It immediately drives business to your website and, ultimately, more money to your bottom line.

Making regular media appearances that you amplify in all the incredible ways that are available to us today can revolutionize your business in ways you can't even begin to imagine. That's what happened for me.

Never before have there been more ways to build a presence that matters.

If you are the executive of a corporation, the author of an upcoming book, the owner of a rapidly growing small business, or the public face of a local nonprofit, if you have a business to build or people you want to help, nothing beats using the media to create the visibility, influence, and power you need.

Are you ready to learn how to make it rain?

CHAPTER 2

Lock On to Your Brand

When I talk to talented people about the incredible opportunity it is to be an expert in demand by the media and how much it can do for their business and their platform, I'm surprised to hear how quickly some of them doubt themselves.

In my experience, a lot of people out there have an expertise, but they don't give themselves credit for it. Other people are comfortable claiming to be experts if they have formal credentials and experience, but they may be overlooking other areas of expertise they've developed over the years. And let's face it—some people profess to be experts, but they are not. They clearly need to spend more time researching and honing their skills.

By all means, look to your career when you're thinking about which expertise to claim as your own, but don't stop there. In TV and the media, experts are called upon to share information on a wide range of topics: terrorism, the economy, the housing boom, aircraft stability, gun safety, parenting, educational policy, the Electoral College, Neighborhood Watch, cooking, landscaping, medicine, fitness—you name it. If it's in the news, there's a producer somewhere looking for an expert. The question is: Will you seize the opportunity?

Start by asking yourself whether you have developed an expertise as defined by one of these three areas:

- **Training and Education:** Professional training and education qualify you to offer an opinion on matters related to your field. Maybe you're a nurse, a psychologist, an accountant, a pilot, a firefighter, a pharmacologist, a professor, a scientist, a programmer, or a florist with years of training and experience. If you don't have the requisite education, there are more options than ever, including online and weekend and evening programs that cater to adults and working professions. Most of these programs offer affordable opportunities to get college and advanced degrees in a range of disciplines. You can even get a law degree or PhD online!

- **Knowledge and Experience:** Sometimes knowledge and experience alone can be enough to qualify you as an expert, regardless of formal degrees or certificates. Think about an electrician with thirty years of experience, or a ship captain who has spent the last six months working in Antarctica, or a dauntless fitness trainer who worked with the athlete no one expected to win in the Paralympics. Wouldn't you want to hear from them if a news story broke in their area of expertise? Think about what you spend your time doing. Have you built up enough knowledge and experience in something to qualify as an expert?

- **Accomplishments:** Regardless of education and training, a serial entrepreneur who has carved out a successful business niche again and again, or a CEO with finely honed insights into leadership and intimate personal knowledge of what it takes to make it to the top, can undoubtedly bring invaluable information to a media conversation. Your own accomplishments and those of your business confer an authority and expertise that have earned you a place at the table.

If you meet the qualifications based on education, training, or accomplishments, you have the expertise that a range of media outlets are looking for. The key is having a clearly identified brand, a concrete strategy, and the commitment to go to the next level.

Understanding Branding

We used to live in simpler times. The only brands most of us knew about were managed by big corporations: IBM, Coca-Cola, BMW. "Personal branding" wasn't on anyone's radar. Selfies didn't exist. If you wanted to build a business, you advertised; you didn't have to strategize about how to keep a conversation going with thousands of strangers online.

If that sounds like a better world to you, you're mistaken. The advantages available to us—for free—in the last decade are so much greater than anything that's ever been possible, the two worlds can't even be compared. Never before have you had the chance to build a personal brand like you can today.

Although 70 percent of professionals think they know their brand and 50 percent believe they are living it, that's not the case. In the *Forbes* article "Personal Branding Is a Leadership Requirement, Not a Self-Promotion Campaign," Glenn Llopis explains that less than 15 percent of all business people have defined their personal brand clearly and not even 5 percent are living it consistently.[1]

What people often mistakenly mean by "branding" is actually "self-promotion." They are simply committed to promoting themselves in any way at any time, rather than zeroing in on a clear brand identity that provides value to others.

Self-promotion is much easier. Crafting a brand requires reflection, strategic thinking, and self-awareness. Promoting it consistently means taking action and being accountable for the results.[2]

Your personal brand should convey who you are and what you represent as an individual and a leader. Your business brand, too, conveys the core of your business, what it represents and the value it brings to your customers.

When you present your brand consistently, people come to know what to expect from you and ultimately look to you for insights and leadership in your niche. A brand gives you a means to earn respect in your field. While it may feel uncomfortable at first to adjust your public actions through the lens of a brand, it will give you a firm foundation to build on. Your message, your choices of media appearances, your posts, your tweets—everything you do to promote your business and brand will rest on that foundation.

That doesn't mean you're acting, or pretending to be someone you aren't. Instead, your brand should allow you to focus on being more of who you naturally are—and, more important, who you want to be—so you can bring your best self when you share your message with others.[3] The more your brand matches who you genuinely are, the more sustainable it will be. Consider it an opportunity to use your own traits and distinguishing characteristics to your advantage.

Robert Reich, the former U.S. Secretary of Labor, is less than five feet tall. For his whole adult life, when people first meet him, they react to his height with stunned silence. There was no way around it. So he took charge of the issue and built it into his brand. Now whenever he appears on stage, he starts with a joke about his stature to put people at ease. It allows him to join them while they take it in. When he wrote a book about the presidential campaign, he led with that aspect of his brand again, naming the book: *I'll Be Short*. By owning this unavoidable part of how people perceived him, he shrewdly leveraged it into his brand.[4]

When space scientist Natalie Starkey appeared as an expert on the BBC after a meteorite hit Russia in 2013, she was part of a new wave of confident women appearing on TV because they recognized that branding is good for business. In "The Rise and Rise of the Female TV Expert," Kirsty Walker describes a wide-range of women who share their expertise on a wide range of shows: volcanologists, geologists, cosmologists, physicists, neuroscientists, anthropologists, and classicists, as well as a racing car stunt driver, a jet pilot, a world backgammon champion, a founder of a chocolate company, and Angelina Jolie's stunt double from the Lara Croft movies.[5]

People often tell me that they can't limit themselves to a single brand because they have so many different interests and skills. The truth is, we all do. There is no reason to think of your brand as your entire personality. It's a useful selection of who you are.

Suppose it were possible for you to appear on *Dr. Phil* this week as an expert on landscaping and next week as a military flight instructor and the week after that as a salsa dancer. Putting your expertise in all those niches on the air might allow you to include more of your life on *Dr. Phil*, but it would confuse people and dilute the message of your brand. Besides that, why would you want to? This isn't show-and-tell. It's an opportunity for you to make rain for yourself or your business.

If the brand you value most is flight instruction, and you have important points to make about the safety standards in small aircraft or a change in regulations that has led to the loss of life, then every time the viewers of *Dr. Phil* see you, you want them to think "military flight instructor"—not: "Isn't he that guy with a trick for keeping ferns alive?" or "That dude's got some killer salsa moves!"

You can't start to create an immediate association with your brand if you're all over the place. Even worse, jumping from one expertise to another can make you seem like a dilettante. Commit to your brand. It will change your life and improve your bottom line.

When I met with Arielle Ford, who has been one of the leading book publicists in the country for almost twenty years, I told her, "I'm an attorney, but I also want to help shape the conversation about women, children, autism, race, and politics."

"Fine," she said. "You will. But first go with what people instantly recognize you as: an attorney." As she explained it, if I started making appearances as a legal expert on the kinds of cases I worked on, I could gradually build out my brand to include my broader range of interests.

It is counterproductive to pitch shows with a long list of things you're an expert in—law, politics, children's rights, special needs issues, parents of children with autism, advocacy, women in business, celebrity divorce, human rights. Harried producers won't take the time to figure all that out. Producers want people they can readily identify and who have a specific topic they can discuss: "Areva Martin, legal expert." Once you've established that, you can let them know there's more.

Establish Your Brand

Arielle's advice was absolutely right. Locking in your brand and pairing it with a coherent story is the first step to being a rainmaker. No one is going to book you on TV, radio, or even podcasts if you don't have it.

It's like that old joke where a woman tells her friend she's dating a new guy. "He's very talented. He's a sailor, a musician, and carpenter—and practically a computer genius!"

"So. Unemployed, then?" her friend says.

A coherent narrative is extremely important. It not only lets people know where you're coming from, but it helps them integrate the other things they know about you, too.

Maybe you started out as a journalist, reporting on the finance industry. That was a great career, but now you're moving in a new direction and you'd like to build your brand in writing about the restaurant world. Your narrative might be: "I used to write about the financial side of many industries, including food.... I realized that my big-picture knowledge of agricultural trends and finance uniquely positioned me to cover restaurants with a different perspective." Just like a job interview, you turn a perceived weakness into a strength. Before people can say, "This guy's been writing about finance for twenty years, what does he know about food?" You take control of the story: "I bring an inside knowledge to the food industry that nobody else has."[6]

Always avoid explaining any brand adjustments in terms of your own interests. Instead of saying, "I got bored with that" or "It wasn't the real me" or "My journey took me down a different path," keep your message on point. It's fine to share your personal journey with your friends, but when you are appearing on behalf of your brand, control the narrative. Emoting about your process may feel cathartic for you, but it does nothing for your message, so leave it out. Take people's attention back to the value your previous experience brings to your brand.[7]

Even millennials who couldn't find jobs after college and ended up flipping burgers can build that into a coherent narrative, if they reframe it as "learning valuable skills on the front line of a customer service organization."[8]

What do you remember most about Nelson Mandela? Most people know that he spent twenty years in prison for his opposition to apartheid, then became the first black president of South Africa. This great, inspiring story was the heart of his brand. Other aspects of his life—his three marriages, seventeen grandchildren, love of boxing, and long-distance running—might have been very much a part of how he thought of himself and his life. But those elements were not related to his brand. Ask yourself which high-profile figures in your brand niche you admire most. Why do you admire them? What story do they tell?

Grow with Your Brand

You can expect the focus and the story of your brand to grow and develop as you go along. I took Arielle's advice and identified "legal expert" as my brand for many years. It opened doors, as she said it would. As time went on, however, I gradually began to comment via social media about other issues, such as women's rights, children's rights, autism, and even pop culture. At first, my comments were closely related to the law, but over time, I was able to expand the boundaries a bit further. My core message is still advocacy because it's my genuine passion, so I never stray too far from a legal perspective on those issues. But eventually I've gone on to be a cohost on a panel on *The Doctors*, a medical show where I routinely talk about a wide range of issues on a weekly basis.

Choosing a narrow brand message gets you in the door. Once you've established yourself, you can look for opportunities to bring other issues in. As you are growing your brand, you can start to think about your passions and hobbies. Growing up with my grandmother, who was wheelchair-bound in a poor community where so many families lacked the basics, inspired me to want to be a champion for the underdog. From as far back as I could remember, I have always been inspired to help vulnerable children and women. I took that into consideration as I started to build my brand out. Now my chyron (the explanatory caption shown at the bottom of the screen on TV shows) identifies me as a "children's rights advocate" or "women's advocate" more often than "legal expert." It's come back full circle to where I began.

Define your brand as clearly as possible, but realize that it's a work in progress.

"Many people ask me how I decided to brand myself as a social media and pop culture expert," my friend Samantha Schacher says. "It did not happen overnight, and was not necessarily a decision, but rather an evolution of passion that stemmed from my work."

In her early days as a commentator and host, she didn't know to hone in on a specific niche, so she followed her own interests in entertainment, pop culture, fashion, gaming, and sports. Only after hosting many shows did she realize that pop culture was the area where she flourished most and got the most engagement from her followers on social media.

"A host or an expert today needs to live, breathe, and genuinely love researching their work," Sam says. "Because the more you know your field, the more informed your opinion will be, and the more others will want to hear what you have to say."

Dr. Drew Pinsky once told me that he had no specific plans to make appearances in the media. While he was still a medical student in the eighties, he was asked to appear on a radio show, where people were calling in with important medical questions about AIDS. Lives were on the line, and he felt an obligation to educate himself and other people about the epidemic.

Intuitively, he believed that, as a doctor, it was his job to educate others about issues that were medically and socially important. For ten years, he saw patients all day, then went to the radio station to answer questions from midnight to 3:00 a.m., while his colleagues were sleeping. He started out appearing on the radio show for free, then ended up getting paid.

After the radio show, he began to speak out about teen mothers who were exposed to trauma. That evolved into interviews about what drives at-risk sexual behavior. By the nineties, that turned into conversations about the epidemic of substance abuse. Running a substance abuse treatment center led to a VH1 show on celebrity rehab, then regular appearances on CNN and HLN as a substance abuse expert.

While he adjusted to the trends taking place in the culture and the marketplace, looking for new places to contribute his expertise, Dr. Drew always stayed close to brand: an abiding interest in human behavior. From the beginning, he has seen his media platform as an opportunity to make a real difference in the world.

As Sam Schacher says, "Focus on the blueprint. Lay the groundwork. Work hard and build, build, build." When you've built a solid brand, booking media appearances will be infinitely easier to do. The key is being tenaciously consistent.

Be Ready

Timothy Snell has styled some of the biggest celebrities in Hollywood, such as Queen Latifah, Angela Bassett, Denzel Washington, and Taraji P. Henson. He styled and traveled for fourteen years with the late Whitney Houston. Throughout these experiences, he never lost his passion for his brand, which he describes as "helping curvy women look and feel their best." For years, he thought women who wore size 14 and above were forgotten in the fashion world, and he wanted to change it.

Timothy's big break came when he was asked to do regular segments on Queen Latifah's nationally syndicated talk show. Rainmaker that he is, he automatically used this precious media time to show the vast audiences that size 14 women could wear the same outfits as a size 2 model.

Not only were these segments a huge success, often rating higher than some of the show's celebrity interviews, but they cemented Timothy's brand as the go-to expert on dressing curvy women. He became known to all in the fashion and lifestyle industry as the expert on making women look and feel their best. As a result, he got scores of new clients, requests for other interviews, print magazine features, and, in 2016, his own fashion reality show on Centric. Timothy was ready!

I wish I could say the same thing about my friend Madison. When she self-published her first cookbook based on recipes from her grandmother that had been passed down for generations, I was excited and so were all of our mutual friends. We eagerly attended her book launch party, as did several high-profile people she had invited to help give the book more visibility. In the end, we had a great time, but the luncheon did very little to promote her book for one reason: Madison wasn't ready.

As we got closer to the event, it was clear that Madison had not clearly identified her brand. I automatically started dropping little posts to heat things up, and that was when I noticed Madison's social media pages. She had no public page for her book, only a personal page with photos of her family and friends—and very little mention of her book at all!

The head shot she sent me to promote the event was another shock. I knew she'd invested a lot of money to hire a big-time photographer, but it was sad to see that photo was completely off message. The lighting was great. Her makeup was pristine. She looked into the camera with focus and intensity. It was perfect for a serious, no-nonsense CEO of a major corporation, not for a master chef.

She had failed to ask so many questions before that photo was taken: What is my brand? How do I reflect that brand? When people meet me, what would they expect me to look like? And who are these people? At the end of the day, I'm trying to sell my book to people who care about what exactly? It's not Fortune 500 companies, where that photo might be appropriate. It's not people who read financial or legal books. In fact, it's not even people who like home makeovers or decorating. It's a cookbook geared toward African-Americans who love traditional soul food but who are also health conscious, so they're interested in recipes that allow them to eat their favorite foods without gaining a ton of weight or elevating their blood pressure.

The African-American demographic likely to buy this book would assume that a woman in a business suit would not be the go-to expert on cooking the dishes they grew up eating at big family dinners or at church outings. In their fond memories of home-cooked meals, their grandmother was not wearing a high-end business suit to crush garlic and dice tomatoes.

Madison doesn't need to try to look like her grandmother, but if her photo doesn't embody the spirit of the book, she's missing the mark for her brand.

When *New York Times* bestselling author Patricia Cornwell's novel *Depraved Heart* came out, it was the twenty-third book she'd written about badass forensic pathologist Dr. Kay Scarpetta. At fifty-nine years old (though she could be mistaken for forty), her press photos show her standing outdoors in a mountain range, wearing hiking gear and camouflage pants, while holding an arrow. When she tells her interviewer, "I can take things that have been traumatic and use them as rocket fuel," you believe her.[9] It's easy to imagine her fearless character as her alter ego. She's sold over 100 million books.[10]

Candace Bushnell, author of the book *Sex and the City*, which led to the six-season-long HBO series of the same name, often poses for photos in short, shimmering cocktail dresses with long flowing hair and six-inch heels. She looks every bit like one of the girls on the show. Her photos match her brand. They say, "When it comes to sex in New York, I know what I'm talking about."

Madison missed the boat with the photo. She missed it with social media, too.

She did hire a videographer to shoot the book-signing party, but the video showed people talking or arriving. It had very little, if any, brand value in the first place. Madison didn't post clips from it to tie it to her message, either.

Her biggest opportunity to convey her message came when she addressed the guests over dessert. Instead of talking about her book, Madison spent the precious currency she had in those few minutes of rapt attention by sharing her own personal journey. Most of us came away with no sense of what set her cookbook apart from all the others. We couldn't even remember her grandmother's name.

Overall, we got a little more sense of who Madison was as a person, but not as an author, and we had no ideas whatsoever about her brand. Most likely, Madison didn't, either.

The point is, you've got to start thinking strategically. Otherwise, the same thing could happen to you. This opportunity fell into her lap. And she missed it.

It's a clear case of not thinking things through, but it's not about being stupid. Madison is a supersmart entrepreneur who has run a successful consulting firm. If she can excel as she does and still miss out like this, any of us can do it. If you are thinking you would never make the mistakes Madison made because you are clear about your brand, great. But if you are one of the 85 percent of the people in the *Forbes* magazine article I cited at the beginning of this chapter, you can learn a lot from Madison's story.

When you are learning the ropes and developing your brand or looking for ways to expand an existing one, look to the experts in your field who have already figured it out. Do an exhaustive audit of their social media accounts; review their websites and blog posts. What articles have they written? What colors are they wearing in the photograph on their book covers? This is the most important time to monitor what the influencers in your field have already figured out. Even if you don't always understand why they're making the choices they make at first, it's safe to assume they've tried a lot of things by now. Emulating them can save you a lot of wasted effort.

In Madison's case, she could have looked to successful chefs who have published countless cookbooks. Famed chef Bobby Flay uses a photo on his Twitter page that has him standing over a stove sipping from a pot. On the cover of his book, *Bobby Flay's Barbecue Addiction*, he has on a casual blue shirt and he is literally flipping meat on a grill. Alice Randall has on a black blouse and is holding a tray of food on the cover of *Soul Food Love: Healthy Recipes Inspired by One Hundred Years of Cooking in a Black Family*.

It may be tempting to assess your brand and the projection of it by checking with your family and friends, but don't rely on their advice—unless they are influencers with an established following and proven expertise within your field. Apart from lacking the knowledge you need to make a good decision on your brand, a good friend is going to try to be supportive regardless of whether your message is on point or not. If you ask them to evaluate a photo, they are likely to base their opinion on how flattering the photo is, not knowing that it could be completely wrong for your brand. Check with people in your industry to see what they're doing instead.

Leverage Your Brand

Leveraging your brand to full advantage—in the media or at events like Madison's book party—requires a new way of thinking. It's not easy. It's taken me years to train my brain to think like this. In Part IV, we'll take a closer look at how to build your social media presence and use it to amplify your media appearances. But here are a few things you should consistently focus on doing:

- Always be on the lookout for opportunities.
- Commit to doing three things a day to promote your brand.
- Amplify every appearance you make with several social media posts.
- Notice how influencers in your field are doing it.
- Audit your brand and how you project it at least quarterly by comparing against competitors and influencers in your field.
- Keep a running list of ideas—even ideas you think of after you've missed an opportunity! There's always next time.

It's human nature to think of some of your best ideas after the fact, but that's a sign that you are thinking like a rainmaker! Write them down and use them the next time!

After Madison's book party, she realized that I could have moderated a panel with her answering questions about her book, or we could have actually staged a cooking demonstration. She could have shot an Instagram video or streamed it on Facebook Live or Periscope. Madison might have set up a red carpet outside and interviewed guests as they arrived: "Lydel just joined us. Did you have a chance to read the excerpt from the book that arrived with your invitation? What did you think? Why do you look forward to reading it?" A thirty-second video clip with a prominent person saying, "I'm excited about reading the book!" is great social media fodder.

At my friend Ginger McKnight-Chavers's book party for her debut romance novel, *In the Heart of Texas*, one of the celebrities who attended was Beyoncé's mom, Tina Knowles Lawson, a media personality, philanthropist, and fashion designer known for the brands House of Deréon and Miss Tina.

Because promoting my brand is like second nature to me now, I made the most of the great conversation I had with Tina. Besides being a lovely person, she was eager to hear more about my work with underserved women and girls, because she had started a non-profit and a group, Tina's Angels, to help middle school girls from disadvantaged communities. I posted a photo on the spot letting both our followers know that we were going to be collaborating on projects together to help young girls, and I tagged Tina.

The unspoken message of the post was: "Here are two influencers coming together to make things happen." Posting "I'm at a party with Beyoncé's mom!!!" is the kind of thing neophytes do all the time on social media. It's not what's done by influencers who are serious about promoting their brand.

To avoid losing out on important opportunities like this, you have to keep the end result in mind. When you go to a convention, a workshop, an event, a trade show, a book fair, or a party on behalf of your brand, make sure you're constantly on the lookout for ways to amplify your message.

You've got to think through all this before the event, before you take your show on the road. You can't start thinking like a rainmaker in the middle of a storm of activity. Be ready.

Build It Out

If you've already established your brand, you can consider bringing in other aspects of your business or your life. You can expand the brand in new directions.

If you don't immediately think "fashion show" when you hear the terms "autism expert" or "social justice activist," you're not alone. Yet 2018 will be the tenth anniversary of the Pink Pump Affair, the charity fashion show for the autism nonprofit I started a decade ago, Special Needs Network.

Empowering women and raising awareness about children with autism and other special needs, as well as my own love of fashion, came together to make this a logical way for me to build out my brand, even if the connection isn't obvious at first.

My ongoing media appearances have raised the profile of this event and its attendees every year. The higher-profile my brand becomes, the easier it is for me to attract top-notch fashion designers, bloggers, actresses, and other celebrities to this event, which in turn attracts more guests and more generous donations. While media appearances are a phenomenal way to revolutionize a commercial business, they can do exactly the same thing for a nonprofit organization.

The key is not only to host a great event but to build it out in as many ways as possible before, during, and after the event.

At a recent Pink Pump Affair, we honored Jamie Brewer, an actress with Down syndrome from FX network's hit anthology horror series, *American Horror Story*, as the new face of beauty. We then had a fashion show for curvy women to celebrate a variety of body types. Journalists were invited to cover the event and write about this important topic.

Earlier that day, I hosted a beauty blogger panel discussion called "The Changing Face of Beauty." The subjects we talked about were ready-made headlines for articles, blogs, and news coverage: What's changed in the last decade? Is there a new standard of beauty? What are the standards of beauty? How is beauty affected by age, hair, body size? How can aspiring entrepreneurs capitalize on the multi-billion-dollar beauty industry?

Afterward, everyone on the panel amplified the event (as I'll be encouraging you to do in Part IV) by posting blogs and articles about it. Every time the bloggers promoted the event to raise awareness for autism, it drove more traffic to the Special Needs

Network site and allowed donors who weren't present at the event to make contributions using an online portal. The Pink Pump has become a mainstay in the Los Angeles business, philanthropy, and entertainment communities, selling out weeks in advance. Using my social media outlets and those of our celebrity guests, we have generated more than eight million impressions and have engaged with thousands of women and men across the country, thereby raising the profile of Special Needs Network while raising much-needed funding for the organization's many autism programs.

I meet a lot of people who are able to use the platform they have built with media appearances to promote a cause that they care about, either directly by speaking out about it or indirectly, by rallying their celebrity friends to raise money for the cause.

TV and movie stars do this all the time. In 2016 Sean "P.Diddy" Combs launched a charter school in Harlem for marginalized and low-income students. Born in South Africa, Charlize Theron uses her high profile to boost her Africa Outreach Project. Kristen Stewart's volunteer work with Shoe Revolt helped draw attention to the problem of sex trafficking in the United States. Alicia Keys's music platform allowed her to magnify her impact as an ambassador for Keep a Child Alive. 50 Cent used his name recognition to raise money for Bringing Positive Change Charity Day.

When you build out your brand at every stage, you will see the opportunities grow beyond anything you imagined starting out. If you do not yet have the name recognition to add value to a cause, making regular media appearances and amplifying them on a consistent basis will help you get there. And with all the different media channels, having name recognition in a particular niche will suffice. It will help you attract potential partners who are most likely to join with you as you promote your cause.

Think big. That's what making rain is all about.

The more you build out your brand, the easier it will be to find people eager to leverage their brand along with yours. If you find that everyone you approach is looking for more "social proof" of your ability to reach a wide audience, then work on building your social media following, while you continue to network and make media appearances.

It's a progression. While I was trying different ways to expand my own brand beyond legal issues, I was also developing my skills at linking everything to my message. Whether I'm talking about celebrities on daytime talk shows or abducted children on *Anderson Cooper 360°*, I never forget my brand and the opportunities I have through philanthropy, civic engagement, political fund-raising, health and fitness, and the range of activities I am involved with that are derivatives of my brand. The key is to use all of the assets you have in establishing your brand: credentials, experience, and accomplishments.

Since attorney Anahita Sedaghatfar started appearing on TV as a legal expert, her opportunities to exploit her brand have grown:

> "There's no doubt my brand has expanded exponentially since I started doing TV. Getting the national TV exposure has not only expanded my law practice but has opened doors for me to work as a public speaker, get more involved in high-profile matters involving the Persian Jewish community, work on podcasts, do pilots for shows, and write articles."

For Samantha Schacher, the experience of building her brand taught her skills that she's using to expand into books, products, and other businesses. With her husband, she has created a candle company, Biren & Co. The experience Samantha has gleaned from selling her brand on TV has given her the skills to launch their products with great success.

Over time her range of expertise in the media has naturally expanded, too. Her original expertise in pop culture has come to include politics as well:

"In this day and age, politics has become pop culture. Our current president is a former reality TV star, and most trending stories today on social revolve around politics, social issues, etc.—it *is* pop culture.

"Because my job is to be in the know on all things trending, I have become well versed in politics and social issues. And because my brand is reliant on an opinion, I can't merely report about Trump's cabinet, or DAPL, or BLM. I need to have an opinion, and I need to be able to assess the reaction and narrative on social.

"I love that my brand has expanded into this territory because, for me, it is very fulfilling to be able to connect with people from all over the world, creating a dialogue on very important issues that affect the U.S. I am a huge advocate for human rights, the environment, animal rights, so you better believe I am going to be well versed and have a voice when it comes to equality, climate change, animals, etc."

So many others have leveraged their media success into product lines and other business ventures. The Jenner sisters developed Kendall + Kylie clothing. Jennifer Lopez launched a perfume brand. Tyra Banks founded TZONE, an organization to help girls from low-income families. Glenn Close started FetchDog, a pet accessory site where she interviews celebrities about their relationships with their dogs. CNN anchor Zain Verjee created a media production company, aKoma, to host and amplify stories about Africa.

The challenge is to be strategic about making sure your initial brand is strong before you build it out in new directions. Avoiding brand confusion is far more important than talking about all your interests. Only when you've established yourself will you have the luxury of moving in new, exciting directions while sticking close to your original message.

Figure out how you want to be perceived. Develop a compelling story that explains your evolution. Then spread the word. The more connections you make, the more engagement you elicit, the more value you bring, the more likely it is that your brand will be rewarded.[11]

"The one thing you have that nobody else has is you. Your voice, your mind, your story, your vision," Neil Gaiman once said. "So write and draw and build and play and dance and live as only you can."

PART II

WHAT YOU NEED FIRST

CHAPTER 3

Find Your People

I'm a news junkie. First thing in the morning, I check my news apps—usually before I have my morning tea. So when I look for people like me, I know they're going to be consuming news, too. They'll care about legal issues, special needs, politics, children's issues, and civil rights. My target outlets will be any place where I can reach those people and help shape the conversation.

Back in the day, the thinking was that you could find your target market by asking questions like:

- Who are you are trying to reach?
- What genre are they?
- How old are they?
- Where do they live?
- What do they do for a living?
- What other aspects of their lives matter?
- Where can you find them?
- Who is your competition?

Are you old enough to remember people saying that the demographic for a particular brand was "18- to 49-year olds"? With the Big Data analytics we all have at our fingertips these days (and the apps to make it simple for us), it's a new era. Lumping your target market into a generic bucket like that today would be like trying to sell your latest hip-hop riff to "people who like music."

The old assumptions have been upended. Very few things—age demographics included—mean what they used to. According to CNN Money, college graduates today "don't just change jobs, they often switch into entirely different industries.... Young Millennials (those who graduated from 2006 to 2010) are on track to surpass four job changes by the time they hit age 32."[1]

It's getting harder to make assumptions based on demographic data any more. One thirty-year-old may be living with his parents, while another is climbing steadily toward the C-Suite. A sixty-year-old might be drinking beer and watching TV in a recliner, or he might be running marathons, cheered on by his second wife and their new toddler. And we know seventy- and even eighty-year-olds are at the highest leadership of the U.S. government.

Media outlets spend a lot of their marketing budget identifying who their target audience is. Before you start choosing the outlets that are most likely to help you make it rain, you need to find out who your people are. Knowing who follows you on social media, who has an interest in your area of expertise, and who is likely to buy your products or service will help you identify the types of shows and media channels you want to target for interviews. Luckily, we live in an age with far more ways to analyze that information than we could ever possibly mine.

Know Your Targets

Who is already following you? Whether you have a solid presence or are just starting to establish one via a website, social media, e-mail lists, or blog, you don't have to guess. You can look at the evidence. Even if you're just starting out or revamping and moving in a new direction, you can ask the same questions of the early people who show up for your brand.

Social

Notice who is sharing your content the most. This can be as simple as monitoring your social accounts to see who is interacting with your content. These are the people you want to reach. They engage your content. Take a look at their bios to see if common interests or qualities emerge.[2]

What type of content is shared the most? Tracking this kind of data can help you hone in on your target audience. You are likely to find, as all of us do, that the type of posts you assumed would be most popular aren't necessarily the ones that generate the most engagement.

Analytics

If you have a growing number of followers on your Facebook page, Facebook Insights will allow you to quickly find out demographic information about your most active users and the topics that they engage most.

You can find it on the top bar of your Facebook Page, where the options are:

Page | Messages | Notifications | Insights | Publishing Tools

As you know, Facebook is always changing. If these options disappear, simply search for "Facebook Insights" to find out where the link has moved. You won't be the only one looking. Click "Facebook Insights." Then click "People." A graphic will appear showing various percentages and categories under: "Your Fans," "People Reached," and "People Engaged."

In 2016 Twitter launched Dashboard, a powerful tool that showed businesses exactly what their followers were interested in, as well as the topics and other Twitter accounts that the followers had in common, but they shut it down after six months. At the time of this writing, Twitter is promising to bring back a new and improved version.

When social media platforms do not provide insightful analytic data, it leaves an unfilled gap in the market. Other businesses usually seize the opportunity to create an app or other software to serve the same function. There are a lot of options out there. My only warning is that following analytics can become addictive. It's wonderful to be able to drill down into the data and find out exactly what's going on, but never forget that understanding your audience is the goal.

E-mail

E-mail allows you to develop a relationship with your target audience in a different way from social media. It gives you an open channel for feedback and a meaningful exchange.

Later in the book I'll say more about the importance of converting as much of your social media following as possible into e-mail lists. Even though people have abandoned e-mail for chatting and messaging, e-mail is still far better for monetizing your brand. If you have any interest in that, don't dismiss e-mail yet!

As you build an e-mail list, you'll want to send out content at regular intervals. It may not be your primary goal, but it's become an important aspect of building a dedicated following. After they have received content for about thirty days, send another e-mail to ask if they're enjoying it. By sincerely soliciting a response, you begin a conversation that can provide you with valuable information about what's working and who your most engaged target audience is.[3]

Survey

The most engaged audiences are happy to participate in surveys from brands they appreciate. For years, Michael Hyatt, one of the most innovative marketers around, ran an annual Reader Survey, often with more than fifty questions. He explained it to his audience this way:

> "I want to make my blog better and more relevant to your needs and interests. To do that, I need to know more about *you*.... Would you please take a few minutes to fill out the survey? By doing so, you will ultimately be helping yourself. Why? Because you will be helping me make my content even more interesting and relevant to you. Your input is important to me."[4]

Along with more than a dozen demographic questions, Hyatt asks how readers like his blog, podcasts, products, conferences, and courses. He even adds questions like these:

- What do you like most about my blog?
- Where has my blog helped you most?
- How can I make my blog better?
- What's the biggest challenge you are facing right now?
- What's your favorite way to learn?
- How many webinars did you attend in the last twelve months?
- What social networks are you active on?

Once the survey results are compiled, Hyatt shares his insights with his readers. His posts initiate discussions that give even more insight into people's answers on the survey and get them engaged with each other. It is a brilliant way to turn a "target audience" into a like-minded community.[5]

Make It Count

When it comes to getting your message out, Jim Sterne, author of *Social Media Metrics*, has it right when he says: "When a tree falls

in a forest and there is nobody there to hear it, it makes no difference whether it makes a sound or not."[6]

If you're not getting your message to the right people at the
right time, why does it matter? A media appearance on a major
network may make a Facebook post to be proud of, but it will be of
little to no substantive benefit to your brand or business—unless
it fits the market.

The question to ask yourself is: Will this make it rain? You've
got to find the outlets your people are going to watch and make your
appearances there. If you're in the wrong venue, you may be having
a great time but you've lost sight of your goal.

Mother's Restaurant has been a New Orleans institution since
it opened in 1938. At lunch hour, it's not unusual for a hungry line to
form outside, while the locals wait to order Mother's unbeatable
po-boys, shrimp creole, and jambalaya. The owner, Jerry Amato,
is fond of saying, "Everybody gets fed. Everybody comes back."[7]

Years ago, Jerry bought out the property next door and turned
it into a banquet hall called Mother's Next Door. It's doing fine,
but the right media appearance could certainly give it a boost. If
Jerry were to seize an opportunity to appear on CNBC talking
about the restaurant industry, he may get an enormous number of
viewers, but the appearance may not have much effect. Some local
viewers who watch CNBC for investment insights may want to
check out the restaurant, but they're not watching that channel for
tips on where to eat, so that appearance isn't going to encourage a
significant increase in the regular and reliable flow of customers.
His efforts would be much better spent appearing on a local affiliate's morning show to highlight a hot new menu item.

When my aunt, Robbie Montgomery, the chef and owner
of two Sweetie Pie's soul food restaurants in St. Louis goes on
national talk shows to promote her famous six-cheese-baked mac-
aroni, she gets a boost from tourists, but it's the local St. Louis
broadcast shows that cause her phones to ring off the hook after

episodes of her cooking demonstrations. The folks in our home-
town of St. Louis stand in line for two hours to eat at her über-
popular restaurants, and although she has been in business for
more than two decades, Robbie's recent media appearances have
made the difference in the success of her restaurants, a cookbook,
and other Sweetie Pie's products.

I know from personal experience. When I sold my second
book, *The Everyday Advocate: Standing Up for Your Child with
Autism*, to a major publishing house, I was ecstatic! Not only did
I get a big advance, I also was going to be able to share my legal
and personal knowledge of autism with millions of special needs
families. To promote the book, I made several TV appearances
on national TV shows, including *Dr. Phil*, *CBS This Morning*,
and *The Doctors*. I also made a ton of TV and radio appearances
on news and lifestyle shows in large media markets like Chicago,
New York, and Boston to check all the boxes. It looked like the
marketing was ideal.

The first week the book was released, it was an Amazon Best
Seller in its category. But it didn't last for long, and I quickly realized that my media strategy wasn't the most effective for a book
about special needs advocacy. The strategy did provide greater
name recognition for my personal brand. It certainly helped me
build momentum that aided me in getting invitations to appear as
an expert on more and more major shows. But it didn't increase
book sales because, as exciting as it was to appear on major shows,
they were not going out to the right demographic for the book.

The target market for *The Everyday Advocate* was the parents
of children with special needs. That's only 15 percent of the parents watching those shows.[8] If I had gone deeper into the special
needs community, 100 percent of the audiences would've been
right for the book.

It's great to reach a national audience, but I should've been
talking at schools, connecting with librarians, doing guest blogs

on websites of influential parents of special needs kids, and making appearances on shows specifically directed to the special needs community. Instead of asking, "How can I get the most viewers?" it would've been better to ask "Where does my target market get their news? Are they much more likely to tune into NPR or CBS? Where can I reach the most people in my specific market niche at one time?"

Ironically, without a clear recognition of your brand and a focused plan, you can miss your mark in the middle of great success. It happens all the time.

With a little effort you can find the perfect media outlet for your brand and expertise. In law, we call that "due diligence." It means doing what you need to do so you'll be fully prepared. In this case, your diligence will really pay off.

Suppose you run a substance abuse treatment clinic in Atlanta. Your programs have had exceptional success with "medically managed withdrawal." In your view, programs across the country would have better long-term results if they used this method. Because of the way this approach has saved patients' lives, you feel passionately about getting the word out. How do you find media outlets to invite you on the air to speak about this subject?

One way is to start with related keywords, such as *substance abuse, opioid crisis, treatment clinic, addiction, rehab, prescription painkillers, alcoholism,* and so on. Google Keyword Planner or Hashtagify can help expand your list.

Use these keywords to search for sites and articles on your browser, for videos on YouTube or Vimeo, and for hashtagged posts on social media in the last six months. The results will tell you exactly what you need to know. Be sure to keep detailed notes. It's going to be a lot of information.

Out of the millions of results, make a list of the media outlets that are covering this topic. The major networks will appear at the top. While it may be appealing to imagine yourself on these shows, they will always be the most competitive and will not necessarily be the best match for your brand, even when you have enough experience with media interviews to warrant their attention.

Cable networks, Internet radio shows, local affiliates, and other outlets will be a few pages further in the search results. These will be the easiest places to start. Build a list of these outlets, watch the shows, then take your research further.

- Study their websites to see what kind of topics they cover. Can you bring a unique angle to their conversation about substance abuse?
- Get to know their hosts. What tone do they establish?
- Observe the guest experts in your field. What are their points of view?
- Identify the five to ten outlets that best match your brand. Which outlets feel like a good fit for both your message and your level of experience in media interviews?
- Look for the producers of the shows at the closing credits, then call the show to confirm their names and contact information.

Another option for finding the best media outlets for your brand and expertise is to get to know the people who regularly appear as guest experts on your topic. Seeing which outlets they frequent will help you cut to the chase. Most experts download videos of their media appearances to their YouTube channel. You will likely find long lists of their articles, speaking engagements, and recent appearances on their websites.

If you are the founder of a cybersecurity firm and a member of the cast on ABC's *Shark Tank* like Robert Herjavec, regular appearances on business and financial shows on CNBC are probably your sweet spot. Conversations about how to prevent cyber attacks on Fortune 500 companies would be of great value to CEOs and CFOs. When my friend, actress Vanessa Bell Calloway, tweets about her upcoming interview on the daytime talk show *Home & Family* on the Hallmark Channel, it makes sense, given that Vanessa produces and stars in a web-based cooking and lifestyle show, *In the Company of Friends*.

Los Angeles political consultants John Thomas, of Thomas Partners Strategies, and Dave Jacobson, of Jacobson & Zilber Strategies, started making regular appearances on the Fox LA affiliate station during the presidential election. John is a Republican strategist and Dave has built his career helping Democratic candidates get elected. You can count on them to take partisan positions, but for local candidates running for office, seeing them on Fox's *Good Day LA* and *Fox LA News at 5* pontificating about breaking political news validates them as trusted political consultants and has caused both to expand their local brand names and grow their stables of clients.

Until recently we didn't have nearly the ability to find out exactly where a target audience is and what they want to hear. Now we can simply ask our people where they get their information and go there.

Between social media analytics and direct engagement with your target market through surveys and e-mail, you can come to know exactly what your followers are thinking and feeling about the issues that matter most to you. If you focus on the people in your audience whose opinions the rest of the audience listens to, you can have an even greater impact.

Influencing the Market

When it comes to rainmaking, not all followers are equally valuable. Some people have a lot more influence than others.

It's great if you get your message to Justin. But it's better if you get your message to Dave, who tells Brianna and Tyler, and

Brianna and Tyler pass the word to influencers, like Daniel, Jasmine, and Jayla. Your message is then magnified at a much greater rate, since influencers have a bigger audience, a greater degree of engagement, and more powerful voices overall.[9]

Amplifying your media appearances and message can happen quickly when you align with influencers. They can garner the attention of their own bigger audience along with that audience's network. The loyalty they've cultivated among their followers can not only drive traffic to your site, it can expand your own following on social media and flat-out sell your products.[10]

One recommendation from someone we trust means more to all of us than a pitch from someone we don't know. Consumers today are blind to billboards and deaf to commercials. When they look into products, services, or businesses, it's because they've heard about it from someone they trust.[11]

Can you even remember the last time a TV commercial came on when you didn't pick up your phone and start checking your messages? We've learned to tune out ads. Promotions are happening on social media, too, but they're brought to us by people we follow, who have learned to stay true to their own unique voice and message, while recommending products and brands.[12]

As a rainmaker, that's what you're going to do, too. This book isn't primarily about the many opportunities available in social media, but if you want to reap the benefits, you need to put it into action and watch closely how the most successful influencers in your niche are doing it. Identifying who they are and developing mutually beneficial relationships with them are important steps. Here are a few ways to do that, but the possibilities are limited only by your imagination.

- Google the top people in your field—for example, "top financial planners" or "top medical doctors."
- Keep a running log of experts in your field when you're engaged with media.

- Identify the top authors in your field on Amazon.
- Follow all these influencers on social media.
- Engage them in conversations with comments.
- Offer something that may be of help to them, such as a link to a related article.
- Follow their followers.
- Follow the people recommended by Facebook and Twitter when you go on those people's social media pages.
- Study their posts for a few minutes every day, making note of the experts they engage.
- Check out speakers bureau websites for speakers in your field.
- Note the experts in your field cited in any articles you read.

Any successful businessperson has the skills to find influencers in their field in minutes.

If you do all these searches, you will be inundated with contacts and leads to follow. Amazon alone has thousands of books in any given field. Within those books are countless references to other experts in the field. The challenge is to shift your mentality to be alert to the scores of influencers you meet, hear about, or encounter in the course of your week.

Once you have built a long list of connections with experts in your field, you can begin to identify which of them are the most influential. Keep in mind that influence is about more than the number of page Likes. It's not enough for somebody to have a million Twitter followers, if they're not highly engaged. Not everyone with a lot of followers has a lot of influence.

Forbes magazine has come up with a formula to use instead of simply looking for people with a lot of followers:

Influence = Audience Reach (# of followers)
                x Brand Affinity (expertise and credibility)
                x Strength of Relationship with Followers[13]

Some people have huge numbers of followers, but are those followers *acting* on their recommendations? Check out the types of posts, tweets, and comments on their social platforms to assess this.

Consider signing up for Klout, a social media analytics website and app that calculates social influence and provides a "Klout Score" from 1 to 100. After a free sign-in on klout.com, an orange box with a Klout Score is shown beside the name of everyone on Twitter. Klout Scores of at least 50 indicate the influencer is "pretty much rocking the social media world." Scores over 63 represent the top 5 percent of social media influencers.[14] Although the scores are inevitably controversial, they are highly respected in many quarters as an indication of engagement and influence.

Even if the brand seems to match your niche, you should also check to see if their followers align with their own brand. Notice whether their followers are fans or work in the same industry. If they don't have influence with your target market, their social media won't help you meet the people you need.[15] Is their specific niche a good fit for your brand?

If you are a doctor specializing in plastic surgery, for instance, the influencers most relevant to your brand will not be specialists in mental health or cancer. Look closely at the conversations. Do they relate to your brand? Even if a doctor shares your specialty, they may be taking the conversation toward economic, legal, or family issues that are unlike your brand.

Once you have found a good match, one of the most important questions is: Are they leveraging social media well? Do you see signs that they understand how to build a platform? If they're not rainmaking by amplifying their own message, they won't be able to help you amplify yours.

An influencer for one brand isn't an influencer for another. Justin Bieber has more than 96 million followers. He's one of the biggest influencers on social media. If you're a computer expert doing interviews about Internet privacy and selling a security software package, getting Justin Bieber to tweet about your software is not going to increase your sales, because his followers are interested only in him and his music.[16]

When you find the influencers who are respected by and genuinely engaged with your own target market in a way that causes them to take action, look for ways to start the conversation and get to know them. It's less about sending them a gift basket than offering them exclusive "inside" information that will increase their own value to their followers.[17]

While the value of traditional marketing continues to plummet, influencer marketing is quickly gaining ground. It is now considered to be one of the most effective ways to attract followers, clients, and customers. As you start to make more media appearances as an expert, your ability to provide valuable information to influencers will grow exponentially. With retweets, reposts, guest blogs, and shares, they bring your message to their loyal following, inserting themselves into the conversations around your brand. Aligning with these influencers before your competition does can make a huge difference in your success at projecting and monetizing your brand.[18]

Where Are Influencers?

With influence marketing on the rise, new websites, apps, and software for finding and evaluating influencers are appearing all the time. I'll include a few suggestions here to get you started, but as usual, when it comes to technology, you have to keep your finger on the pulse of the Internet to keep up with the latest innovations.

BuzzSumo

BuzzSumo.com provides an advanced social search engine to show you the most shared content for any author, topic, or website. It then shows exactly how often this content was shared on all the major social platforms. So you can assess for yourself how engaged an influencer's followers are.

You can also use BuzzSumo to find trending content to share with your own followers. Looking at what content resonates with the biggest influencers in your niche will tell you where the conversation is going, which can help you find a way to jump in and add value.

Once you explore BuzzSumo, be sure to set keyword alerts when the influencer or your competitors publish a breakout post.

Followerwonk

Focused entirely on Twitter, Followerwonk will tell you about your own followers—where they're located, and what time of day they tweet. It also allows you to connect with influencers in your niche.

Take the time to explore Followerwonk. It has so many options. You can even sort all your Twitter followers by name, tweet count, or number of days on Twitter on a colorful spreadsheet.

#Hashtags

Identify trending hashtags and follow them. When you track these conversations, you can quickly find the people who are the most influential. You'll see their relevant blog posts, their level of engagement, and the fit for your brand.

Using the hashtags on your own posts is a perfect way to jump into the conversation with influencers and potential followers. It can also send your own engagement through the roof.

This is particularly effective when tweeting about shows or events. Shonda Rhimes and the cast of her ABC hit dramas on Thursday nights often tweet using the #TGIT for her popular shows *Scandal*, *How to Get Away with Murder*, and *The Catch*. Those tweets generate thousands of retweets and Likes. If you are a celebrity news junkie, a TV critic, or an agent, what a great conversation to jump into! Even a media-savvy political consultant may want to jump into a conversation about Olivia Pope and her White House drama.

Google Alerts

Setting alerts for keywords related to your brand allows you to follow the conversation taking place, but it's also an invaluable way to find influencers in your niche. Who is speaking up regularly on this topic? When you check their social platform, how high is their engagement on this topic with their followers?[19]

Influencers are seen as thought leaders in their niche. They have privileged access to something everyone else wants: people's attention. That makes them highly valuable, not just to their own followers and their bottom line, but to other thought leaders as well.[20] More and more people are coming to realize what an incredible opportunity it represents.

Studies show that 84 percent of marketers plan to run an influencer marketing campaign during the next year. Influencer marketing will continue to increase. This is just the beginning. It makes you wonder what's next as we all learn new ways to amplify our messages.[21] I can guarantee you it will have to do with greater engagement between influencers and the people listening closely to their message.

Joining the online conversation taking place 24/7 in your own field puts you in an ideal position for becoming an influencer yourself. If you build on those conversations with everything you learn in this book, you will create an influx of new life, people, and ideas into your business. What emerges from that dynamic exchange will bring you a constant stream of opportunities that you could never have expected to create in the old way of doing business.

CHAPTER 4

Hone Your Pitch

R emember the thirty-second elevator pitch? This isn't it. Pitching for media interviews has to be far more specific and creative than that. You're not going to be coming up with a generic pitch that you can use on anyone, anywhere, if you happen to find yourself in a small, enclosed space together. To get on TV or radio, you've got to pitch like a pro.

The fact that there's a twenty-four-hour news cycle means the competition producers face on every show is intense. If you come up with anything generic, they've already heard it. It's going to take a lot more than that. What are you adding to what they've already got—a new perspective, new information, new interpretation? How are you advancing the story?

Breaking news shows are produced daily and they air live. Every morning the producers try to figure out the top news stories of the day. If you want to jump onto that moving train, you've got to get up to speed.

Your pitch needs to stand out, because the producers' number one goal is to make their show stand out. Remember shows that stay on the air do so because of high ratings and commercial buys. This is at the top of every producer's mind. If you've got a hook and talking points that will deliver, you'll have their undivided attention—but only if you've matched your pitch to the right show.

Find the Fit

"I've always considered myself to be just average talent," Will Smith once said. "What I have is a ridiculous, insane obsessiveness for practice and preparation."

When you do your homework, you know which pitch is right for which show. It's hard to imagine producers at ABC's *World News Tonight* leading with the story, "Former Bachelorette Opens Up About Decision to Freeze Her Eggs."[1] The daytime audience that loved that story on ABC's *Good Morning America* would not necessarily tune in to CNN's headline on *Anderson Cooper 360°*: "Coast Guard and TSA Could Face Deep Budget Cuts."[2]

Daytime and nighttime news are very different. There are major variations between shows on the same network. Whatever the show or the venue, each one has its own style and tone, its own audience and point of view. Not only that, you've got to watch the show to hear what they've been saying on this story. You can't go on and parrot what they've already been saying. That's why you've got to be ready.

Stay on top of it. Shows change constantly. Producers, an ambitious breed, are always looking for ways to improve and move up. If you watched a show two months ago, it may have had a different producer with a different agenda. The winning elements of the show will stay the same, but the details that you need to know are subject to change.

Watch TV daily. Target the shows that are most relevant to your brand. Record samples of these shows so you can study them. Notice as much as you can:

- How much time are the guests given to speak?
- Can you identify the talking points of the guests?
- What do guests do or say that you like/dislike?
- How does the host set up the questions?

- Do the guests pivot when they answer to stay on message? If so, what words do they use to make that shift?
- What style of clothing is used on the segment?
- Are lightheartedness and humor appropriate?
- If you were answering exactly the same questions, what would you say?
- Can you fit your talking points into the time allotted to the guests?

This investment of time is indispensible. To make the most of the opportunity to put your brand and message in front of thousands or even millions of people—with the endorsement of TV hosts they know and respect—you need to develop an expertise in your target shows. It's a part of your continuing education.

Beyond that, producers are constantly looking for new types of segments and new ways to engage the audience. Dr. Travis Stork started *The Doctors* ten years ago wearing blue scrubs to reflect his role as an emergency room doctor. As the show has moved away from a focus exclusively on hardcore medical topics to include more current news and pop culture stories, Dr. Travis is regularly in dark denim jeans and a casual sweater. A popular host's change in wardrobe can cause a show to attract new viewers and increase ratings.

Social media and analytics have given networks the ability to instantly measure the success of a segment. So they can try something and analyze the results, and if it didn't get a great response on social media or the numbers they were hoping for, they try something else.

One day my local Fox affiliate suddenly changed the style of clothing the male hosts wore, from open shirts with khakis and a blazer to two-piece suits with button-down shirts and ties. If a new producer takes over a show or marketing demographics indicate that the viewing audience has changed, the dress code will change along with it.

A show may start out with female hosts and guests in slacks and a casual blouse, then inexplicably change to dresses with more jewelry and matching jackets. If I don't make it my business to watch the show before I appear, I can easily show up over- or underdressed!

As I said earlier, news directors are ratings driven. It's like a coach for a sports team. If the team doesn't win, the coach gets fired. These news directors are under tremendous pressure to get ratings, so they are constantly tweaking everything. They may like adversarial debates between two guest experts, but if the audience doesn't like it, that entire element may be gone in two weeks. If you think you've got it bad trying to adjust your tone to their changing styles, just be glad you don't have the nonstop stress of being a news director or producer!

This is why your pitch should always be brief. Producers get tons of pitches every hour and every minute of the day. They need a short, clear pitch. They don't have time to read a dissertation. If you send a long e-mail with bright red lettering and yellow highlighting, it will actually come across as offensive. It shows a lack of respect for the demands on the time of the producer reading it—most likely on their cell phone. And it reads "amateur."

No attachments will be opened. If you forget to include your contact information, they will not come looking for you. Getting an invitation is about making the producer's job so easy that they know you don't need hand-holding. You'll be good to go from the moment when you walk in. They won't have to spend a lot of time prepping you, explaining the topics, telling you who the anchor is, or what they like to see on the show. You're ready.

Of course, you can't possibly anticipate what changes the show might make to their style or format next. No one can. The important thing is to prepare as best as possible, then cut yourself a little slack. You won't get it perfect every time. Sometimes, even when you nail it, the producer won't call—for any one of a hundred different reasons. Remember, becoming a sought-after media expert and influencer is more of a marathon than a sprint.

If you find out all you can about what the shows need, it will have a cumulative effect that's beneficial. You're developing an expertise in providing commentary in the media that can help increase your business and promote your brand.

The more you educate yourself about your target shows, the more you'll begin to think like a rainmaker who truly understands the power of the media to amplify your brand. Soon you'll know more about the media outlets that fit your brand than anyone else appearing on your targeted shows. No matter what changes the latest producers or directors make, you'll know exactly what's been happening with the show. Being well-informed will significantly improve your odds of success.

What you may not hear about until later is that the producers are starting to notice that you're bringing good ideas, you're getting the pitches right—your pitch sounds like it would work on the show, even if they've already put another expert in the slot. Your efforts to inform yourself about your target shows are never wasted, and your level of preparation will cause you to stand out with producers and bookers.

I met executive producer Ianthe Jones when she was a senior producer on *Dr. Phil*. She was assigned to produce the show that launched my book, *The Everyday Advocate*. Recognizing the incredible pressure she was under producing the number one daytime talk show on TV, I made her job and that of her associate producers easier by providing them with tons of information on autism, potential guest experts for the show, different angles to address, and even families who had kids on the autism spectrum that I had worked with in writing the book. From that experience, Ianthe and I became friends. As she moved on to produce other talk shows—from the reboot of the *Rikki Lake Show* to the *Queen*

Latifiah Show—she always called me when the show needed a legal expert, a women's advocate, or a children's rights advocate. As they say, you need to "stay ready, so you don't have to get ready."

Set Yourself Apart

If you watch a story develop and you have an opinion that's contrary to what's being said on the show, that's your hook. If your pitch is solid, the producers at MSNBC will consider that an interesting point of view. A lot of stations like to bring on countervailing points of view. It keeps them from appearing biased and makes for a more engaging show. Your hook might be:

> Contrary to what your anchors have stated, the judge's decision in this case was wrong and here's why: [three talking points].

Because I often have strong opinions and I'm happy to speak out, I've been on a lot of shows where the host introduces me by saying:

> "Many in the news have agreed. Next up, legal expert Areva Martin, who disagrees with the judge's decision. She'll tell us why here."

It's crucial to know who you're pitching and find ways to set yourself apart, but you have to be consistent. You can't be for campaign finance reform on one show and against it on another, just to be a contrarian or to be booked on different shows. People will only start to seek you out and follow you if they know what you stand for. I have turned down offers to appear on shows that have asked me to take a position contrary to what I believe.

During the high-profile murder trial of George Zimmerman following the shooting death of Trayvon Martin, I was frequently asked to appear on shows and to support the position of the defense attorneys. I declined the offers because I had spent months posting on social media and appearing on other shows arguing in favor of Zimmerman's prosecution. There would be no way I could switch positions and maintain any credibility.

What to Look For

Record a segment of each of your target shows. Watch it over and over again. Make yourself an expert on the way this show works.

All shows have their own style. Most local news stations are not opinion driven and don't lean right or left. They do their best to provide the facts. When you go on, the host will say, "Tell us what happened." They may ask, "What do you think this means?" But more likely, they invite historians or experts in the field on the show to provide information, not opinions. They want someone who can explain the facts to the layperson.

Some shows like conflict. I could always count on a spirited debate when I appeared on Dr. Drew's HLN daily talk show. The show always interviewed experts before air time to ensure that they had conflicting opinions and were prepared to defend them.

Others present a certain point of view. CNN, for example, likes to be right down the middle on an issue. Rarely do they cover a news story with a single expert taking one position. Although the executives and anchors have a liberal bent, CNN prides themselves on objective reporting that tells both sides of a story.

If you watch closely, you'll notice that MSNBC doesn't use a lot of practicing lawyers as legal experts. Experts on their shows tend to be law professors or former judges. There are some exceptions. I have appeared on several of their morning and midday news shows. *All In with Chris Hayes* and *PoliticsNation with Al Sharpton* are two examples. But when MSNBC reported on the White House travel ban, the experts were former attorney generals. Although they did have practicing lawyers from the American Civil Liberties Union, they were directly involved in efforts to block the ban. Somebody has made an executive decision to go with professors, while CNN, HLN, and Fox routinely use practicing attorneys as guest experts.

Obviously, if you're a legal expert and practicing attorney, this is something you need to know before you pitch. Not only does it save you time pitching an unlikely venue, you may still decide that your pitch enhances the story enough that MSNBC could invite you on anyway. But at least when you pitch, you'll know it's a long shot. And if they don't call you, you'll know it might have had nothing to do with the quality of your pitch, but more to do with high-level mandates from the executive production team.

But what if your area of expertise isn't a good fit for breaking news? Let's say you're a home decorating expert. You might pitch *Home & Family* on the Hallmark Channel or *Good Morning America*. Both shows have lifestyle segments. But there are important differences that you will discover only by watching the shows carefully.

Morning shows have hours to work with and they each organize their segments in unique ways. When *Good Morning America* airs at 7:00 a.m., they spend the first hour on breaking and more serious news. Businesspeople turn the news on while they're getting ready for work. They want to know the headlines before they start their day. Every hour after that gets progressively lighter. By 9:00 a.m., the demographic has totally changed. Most businesspeople are at work. Most stay-at-home moms or dads have gotten the kids off to school. This audience is much more interested in lifestyle and celebrity stories, which is why in this hour you will see cooking demonstrations, home makeovers, celebrities promoting books and movies, and human-interest stories.

By contrast, *Home & Family* maintains a light tone throughout. When you watch the show carefully, you'll notice that each guest segment is longer than on *Good Morning America* and that they often have six guests integrated throughout the entire show. The book author stays around to chat and make pasta with the celebrity chef and hear garden lighting tips from the landscape architect. Viewers get the feeling that they're at a small but very enjoyable party among friends. If you appear as a guest on *Good Morning America*, you will have a three- to five-minute segment, much like you would have on the evening news. You won't be hanging around to chat with the others.

This is true of *The Doctors*, too. Now that I'm a cohost, I'm regularly in all segments, but when I first started appearing on the show, as a guest expert, I sat in the audience in the chair provided for the visiting experts. When it was time for my segment, the hosts engaged me in the audience for a few minutes, then the cameras returned to the hosts while a producer came and escorted me offstage so the next expert could be brought onstage. It's an efficient approach that shows respect for your time and reflects the format of how they present their content. You're only there while you're sharing your talking points. Though, obviously, a show where you hang around to chat with the hosts and other guests like friends has advantages, too.

The important thing is to know what to expect so you can be prepared. As ridiculous as it sounds, I meet people all the time who don't appreciate the value of studying a show. Many times, people don't even watch a show before they pitch it! It's an amateurish approach. If they wing it like this and do get on a show, it's nothing but luck. Professionals who are serious about building their profile and business don't rely on that. Luck isn't sustainable.

To learn all you can about a show you have targeted for pitching, here are a few things to focus on:

- **Website.** Go to the show's website. Read what they have to say about their own show. How do they think of themselves? What are their goals?
- **Anchors.** Know the anchors. How long do they talk before they ask a question? What types of questions do they ask? How do they speak to the other hosts and experts?
- **Content.** Notice whether the show is opinionated or informational. Are the hosts chiming in with their own points of view, or are they trying to be objective? Has the producer brought on experts who argue or present information calmly?
- **Length.** Time the length of expert segments. How much time do they give the guests to answer? Do they ask follow-up questions? How many talking points do the experts have time to get in?
- **Host Style.** What do the hosts and experts wear? Do they speak formally or informally? Are they smiling or remaining serious?
- **Transitions.** What are the gracious little things they say on the show when they welcome a guest, go to a commercial break, and introduce a new guest? Are they constantly thanking people? Have they inflated the number of times they repeat each other's names? It's subtle, but the more you can match this behavior, the more you'll feel like a fit for the show.
- **Experts Like You.** Pay attention to the types of experts. What kind of credentials do they have? Do they appear regularly on the show (check their websites and social media pages)? Do you notice a pattern? Specifically look for interviews with experts in your niche on the show. How are you different/similar? What are their talking points? What do

you like/dislike about their interview? What would you have said in their place? What can you learn?

- **Producers.** As the credits roll at the end of the show, pause the recording to take down the names of the producers of the segment most related to your brand. Most segments have different producers. On some shows, the credits don't distinguish between production teams for each segment. In that case, it's best to simply call the show and ask.

Naturally, there are many more things to notice as well. The goal is to know your top target shows inside and out. Everything you learn will improve your pitch to the show and your appearance on the show. It's work up front that will increase your chances of success.

Types of News Stories

In news parlance, there are A stories, B stories, C stories, and evergreen stories. It is critical to know the difference as this too will inform your pitching strategy.

A stories lead the news. All breaking news stories qualify. B stories may be related to the A story, but they are not the main headline. C stories garner even less attention at the top of the news than B stories, whether they relate to the main headline or not. Evergreen stories focus on topics that generate ongoing interest and are not date or time specific.

When Adele won the Grammy for Album of the Year on a Sunday night in 2017, she used much of her time onstage to gush about Beyoncé. "I can't possibly accept this award, and I'm very humbled, and I'm very grateful and gracious, but the artist of my life is Beyoncé." Backstage she told reporters that "a piece of me died inside" when she realized that she had won the award instead of Beyoncé.[3]

Beyoncé's snub by the Grammys was the A story on the news

Sunday night and all day Monday. I was writing about it on my blog before breakfast the next morning, but by Tuesday, it was over. If I wanted to write about it, I needed to find an angle that wasn't so Grammy specific. In less than forty-eight hours, that A story was old news. So was the B story about the lack of diversity at awards shows and the C story about what people wore to the Grammys. If you wanted to bring in an evergreen angle, you could comment on the history of the Grammys. Or as a music expert, you could make observations about the changing trends among the types of music that have won Grammys over the years. But the window of time is very short.

Another scandal erupted at the Oscars that year when Karl Lagerfeld accused Meryl Streep of backing out on a $100,000 Chanel gown he'd made her for the Oscars, when someone else offered a cheaper gown, and Meryl Streep fought back. She was livid and demanded an apology. She accused Lagerfeld of ruining her evening on the very night when she was celebrating being the most nominated woman in film with her twentieth nomination.

Lagerfeld's accusation, Streep's reaction, and Lagerfeld's apology held the news as an A story for twenty-four hours. The B and C stories were about the fashion industry. Do the major fashion houses give $100,000 dresses to celebrities? Can the celebrities keep them? What's in it for the house? What about the diamonds actors wear? Are those donated, too? What kinds of agreements are made? Who wore the most expensive gown? Who looked the best on the red carpet? Do the gowns actors wear at the Oscars affect their careers? How does being on the best-dressed list affect the film roles they're offered? Why is it important to spend so much money on stylists, gowns, jewelry, hair, and makeup?

A feud between the most nominated actress in history and the House of Chanel is a much sexier story than the arrangements made between actresses and designers or the machinations in their careers, but the B and C stories allow the networks to keep the A story in play.

Some shows cover only the B and C stories. When Dr. Drew had his daily talk show on HLN, most of the stories he discussed with his panel of guest experts were the B and C stories. They were not the A stories that you could expect to see on the various CNN shows. While the CNN shows were exclusively focused on the latest breaking news related to the 2016 U.S. presidential election, for instance, Dr. Drew and his panel were often discussing viral videos, mysterious murder cases, and teachers behaving badly in the classroom. All of these stories had made headlines in some media outlet, but they were not the lead stories on big outlets like the *New York Times*, *Washington Post*, *USA Today*, or even the *Huffington Post*.

It's critical to know if a show you are pitching focuses on A, B, or C stories. This will help you in defining your pitch and creating unique talking points. Knowing if a show does only evergreen stories is also important. In that case, the producers will be looking for those stories that will be of interest to their audiences indefinitely. They may decide that Meryl Streep's Oscar feud with Lagerfeld is too time and date specific, whereas a story about how designers find their inspiration for Hollywood galas and events is timeless.

Think Beyond Network Media Outlets

As you're putting together your pitch, keep in mind that there are almost countless places for you to pitch. Network news is definitely not the best outlet for many guest experts.

If you're a history professor with a specialty in computer sciences, your ideal audience may be watching the Computer History Museum channel on YouTube. It doesn't reach as many millions of people as CNN, but it has fifty-five thousand active viewers, which may allow you to reach more computer history buffs than you could on any given CNN show. Since it's so closely targeted to your expertise, it's more likely that you could make contacts that are relevant to your brand, get invited back more often, and have an opportunity to speak about more of the topics that you care about. As I said earlier, it's not all about volume. Never underestimate the value of finding your people.

Daytime television routinely covers lifestyle stories, like better ways to organize your home. When it comes to these lifestyle stories, two things are certain: (1) they are evergreen topics relevant to human beings everywhere; and (2) you will not be able to compete with famous, best-selling authors who specialize in your niche. Fortunately for you, daytime television has competition, too. There are myriad other outlets that you can successfully pitch.

Let's say your brand is keeping a home orderly and today. But there's a new book out by Marie Kondo, an organizing consultant in Tokyo who has sold millions of copies of her books in more than thirty countries and was listed as one of *Time*'s "100 most influential people." Tough competition. When she is making the rounds of the talk shows to discuss folding techniques, it's best to either save your own folding pitch for later or simply pitch different shows—including DIY podcasts, YouTube channels, and cable shows.

Before you do, make a point to jot down all the places that have invited Marie Kondo to appear on their shows. These are shows that like to do segments about folding! If you were wondering, now you know. She has done you a favor by identifying them. Granted, the producers will always prefer megastar folders, but they won't always be able to book them and they'll still have air time to fill. In Part III we will talk more specifically about the different media channels available beyond mainstream network news.

Stay as informed as you can be. But be ready to pitch boldly. You never know when the timing might be perfect.

Make Your Pitch

The elements of your pitch are simple: hook, who you are, talking points, call to action. Brevity is key. (One sentence can seem long on a cell phone.) But pack as much punch into each element as you can.

Hook

Your hook should be a very strong opinionated statement to catch their attention. Strong opinions make great TV. Let them know you've got one.

- "Following the death of our son, Travyon Martin, we're now considering a run for political office."
- "Confirmation of Betsy DeVos as Secretary of Education is disastrous for poor minorities and students with special needs."
- "Salacious text messages sent by Baylor University coaching staff are damning to the defense of the victim's lawsuits in the sexual assault claims."
- "Don't count on black voters to show up in the 2018 midterm elections."
- "While U.S. focused on the loss of manufacturing jobs, thousands of retail stores have closed, resulting in millions of lost jobs."
- "Salaries of female CEOs continue to lag behind their male counterparts because male corporate board members judge women more harshly."

Who You Are

Explain briefly who you are and why you'd add real value to the show. If you have unique credentials or the inside story, this is the place to say so. They might not read further. Assume you've got about thirty seconds. It may even make sense to put it in the subject line:

- "Iraqi War Veteran Speaks Out on..."
- "Helicopter Pilot Says Crash Should Never Have Happened"
- "Plastic Surgeon Explains Why Most Breast Implants Don't Cause Cancer"

Talking Points (3–5)

After paying close attention to the length and type of talking points being used on your target show, include three to five equally compelling talking points.

On the air, the best media savvy experts explain things: "Here's what happened and here's what you really need to know." If you make the meaning clear, it will distinguish you from the competition and catch the attention of producers when you make your pitch. Think about what you want the audience to take away from the interview. What are the one or two sentences that the show and anchor feel are the most persuasive or poignant summary of your position? Those sentences will often be the ones tweeted by the show or anchor.

When the assassination of the Russian ambassador to Turkey in an art gallery in Ankara is caught on tape, it's breaking news around the world. A few hours later, another terrorist attack hits the Kurfürstendamm Christmas market in Berlin. People around the world start asking what it means. As an expert, your talking points may be:

- The terrorist attack hours later in a Berlin Christmas market is part of a series of attacks over two days in Ankara, Berlin, Yemen, and Zurich.
- More than any other nation, Turkey knows the pain of assassination: Turkish diplomats have been systematically assassinated by Armenian extremists for twenty years.
- It's not personal revenge, but a strategic campaign.[4]

Call to Action

Briefly let the producer know that you're available and invite them to call you. Never forget to include your contact information.

Let's look at how all these elements come together in a single pitch. Suppose you know of a danger that has been overlooked by the local program talking about summer hiking in the nearby mountains. Your pitch might look something like this:

> Severe risk of poison oak for hikers on specific trails of the Pacific Crest is directly related to cuts in the federal EPA budget. Expect hundreds to be hospitalized with serious injuries as a result.
>
> I am a director of the local Sierra Club and a physician and have been leading hikes on these trails for twenty years.
>
> What viewers need to know:
>
> - At the second ridge, an infestation of poison oak has contaminated the trail. Local authorities are working hard to eradicate it, but this is the worst year yet.
> - Local authorities claim they have been unable to clear the crest of this deadly poison due to recent cuts in the federal EPA budget that caused local communities to lose millions in funding.
> - The Sierra Club is warning members throughout the county to avoid the Crest and to stage protests of the budget cuts.
> - In my medical opinion, anyone who comes into contact with the poison ivy is in danger of serious and life-threatening injuries that could result in weeks of hospitalizations and tens of thousands of dollars in medical expenses.
>
> My press kit is attached to this e-mail. I'm available for interviews. Please give me a call.
>
> [Your Contact Information]

Improve Your Pitch

Once you've crafted your pitch, go over it again. Every pitch you send is a potential media appearance that can bring great value to your business and brand. It's worth the extra effort.

Every great pitch resonates with both the heart and the head. The best experts and influencers know how to make us *care* about the facts. Look for ways to increase its emotional appeal. Highlight what is touching in the story. Point out the areas that people are likely to relate to most. Whether you're commenting on a human-interest story or explaining the technical elements of an airplane malfunction, make them care.

Sharpen your pitch with facts. Experts always bring in interesting facts that the listeners didn't know. Add specific facts to your pitch. Keep each of them short. Recently I saw a former member of the United States National Security Agency talk about an ongoing story involving the investigations of President Donald Trump's 2016 campaign. I had watched multiple shows on this day and had seen at least five guests pontificate on the issue. I was starting to feel frustrated that I was not learning anything new. Each person was basically repeating the same information without adding any new details.

Expert number six got it right. He explained the differences in the House, Senate, and Department of Justice investigations. He also provided a critical piece of new information: Convening an independent commission to investigate the allegations would pose significant issues, since the members would not have access to highly classified intelligence documents and information. This is not intuitive nor is it common knowledge. The other guests had all talked about the need for an independent committee, but never explained the pros and cons.

Make it personal when you can. Having a personal connection to a story can catch producers' attention. You can enhance that connection by contacting people before you make the pitch. Since I grew up in St. Louis, I had a personal connection to the community when the Ferguson police shooting of Michael Brown hit the news. Before I made my pitch, I spoke to people in the area to inform myself about the local reaction. When I pitched the story, I knew what people were saying on the ground and had personal contacts ready for the producer to bring in. It helped significantly as producers love the human-interest / man-on-the-ground perspective. Sometimes they bring in actual eyewitnesses to events, but the next best thing is someone that has talked to witnesses. Never interfere with a story or investigation, of course, but do make personal contacts whenever you can.

Remember that the possibility of a media appearance is not a guarantee. Don't take rejection personally or let yourself get discouraged when you don't get the call. You don't stop being a sales person because one sale falls through. I spent hours on TV talking about the deaths of Eric Garner, Michael Brown, and Trayvon Martin, but there were many more hours of coverage that I didn't participate in. Not every show will want you. That's never going to change. But it doesn't mean there aren't audiences that would love to hear what you have to say. Assume they're out there and keep at it.

Then get ready. Once your pitch lands you a call from a producer or booker, they'll want you at the station right away. This is how it works every day with great, timely pitches. It can happen to you, too. Remember, success is not about winning every time. The only difference between trying and succeeding is persistence.

Tone Matters

Whether you have a track record of media appearances behind you and are ready to pitch to a major TV network or you are making your first media appearance, your pitch will be the same. In some cases, you will need to adjust the tone to match the show. An evening news show may require a more formal tone than a daytime talk show, which is chattier. A live stream may be targeted to millennials who prefer a more hip, casual banter. Podcasts and YouTube shows can have any number of different tones. The substance of the pitch may stay exactly the same, but the research you do to decide which shows to pitch to will let you know how to tweak your pitch to match the show's tone.

It's also true, of course, that after you've worked for a while with the producers of any show, you may develop a strong enough rapport that you can call them up with a quick idea, instead of making a formal pitch, but that can take years. In the meantime, write the best, most compelling pitch you can, every single time.

Let's look at an example of how this works. Imagine you're a professor on a mission to encourage millennials to register to vote in local and national elections. When the story breaks that voting fraud may have led to a millennial's supported candidate for Congress losing a recent election, you feel strongly that the news might have an adverse impact on positive voter registration drives you have been promoting. You've got the credentials, hook, and talking points to back it up. Now what?

Initially, you target two of the top YouTube news outlets that reach a younger demographic: Vice News (2.2 million subscribers) and the Young Turks (3.3 million subscribers).[5] Because Vice is one of the fastest growing channels on YouTube, you know it will reach your ideal audience. A pitch that producers at CBS might think is genius will never cut it at Vice. The tone has to be edgy, hip, with a spin that adds a little fun. Your talking points may be exactly the same, but the way you write the pitch? Totally different.

The CBS show may be more interested in the changing roll of college professors and how inserting themselves into politics may impact college fund-raising and even admissions. Stressing this additional point in your pitch will be important and citing data would be helpful. For Vice, your talking points may focus exclusively on the celebrity influencers who are supporting your effort and how they are using their expansive social media accounts to help bring attention to the issue.

The Young Turks (TYT) presents another challenge: dozens of web series to choose from. They do political interviews on *TYT Politics*, *TYT Interviews*, *The Undercurrent*, *twenTYTwelve*, and *The Point*. Tailoring your pitch to each show will require yet another shift in tone and angle. Your brand, your message, and your own basic point remain the same, but you need to convey it in the vernacular of each show.

Imagine the following pitch for the Young Turks:

Hook

Chance the Rapper & Jay Z #RocktheVote on major cross-country tour

Who You Are

I am Robert Johnson, the youngest college president of a major university. With a core of hip-hop stars to join me, I'm launching a tour to more than forty colleges and universities in thirty states to right this wrong. Together we will slap back at haters who blame college students for creating fake voter registration cards and committing voting fraud in recent Congressional Elections.

Talking Points

1. Chance the Rapper and Jay Z join together to bring out 10,000+ to #RocktheVote, using their outsider status to get insiders to hear the message.

2. Johnson is fully prepared to "whip" and "nae nae" to get the word out. Migos, Little Yatchy, and French Montana may roll through his stop in the ATL.
3. The tour is slated to be one of the biggest political turn ups ever.

Call to Action

Available in studio or on the road, I am ready to bring the Young Turks in on exclusive interviews with the artists and students making it happen.

CBS This Morning has an older demographic. Migos and Little Yatchy might be less exciting to producers of that show than the fifty-year anniversary of Fleetwood Mac.

Hook

At a jazz festival, fifty years ago a new band came out onstage in England for the first time. Nobody had ever heard of Fleetwood Mac. Today they've sold over 100 million records.

Who You Are

Chet Nichols, a sound engineer from the early days in Windsor, England, where Fleetwood Mac got their start.

Talking Points

1. Memories of behind-the-scenes moments on that first appearance.

2. How the dynamic of the band has changed over the years as music and audiences have changed along with it.
3. What gave Fleetwood Mac staying power all this time.

Call to Action

I am available to appear in the studio, by Skype, or by phone to help celebrate fifty years of one of the greatest bands in our history.

Who Makes the Pitch?

The short answer is: You do. You're not in the media in the same way as an actress or A-list celebrity. Most of the time, you're going to do your own pitching.

Occasionally you may hire a publicist to see if they can assist you in developing relationships with specific producers or introduce you to certain shows. A publicist usually charges a monthly retainer. Depending on the market, their fee may be as little as $1,500 or as high as $10,000 a month. If you have an ongoing contract with a public relations firm, they may make your pitches, but most likely, it'll be on you.

I'd recommend that you wait to hire a publicist until you've started appearing on shows and you're ready to take it to the next level. (You'll find more on how to work effectively with a publicist in Chapter 7.) Again, broad national shows may not be an improvement for you. It depends on your brand and your goals. There is no one path for success. Many of the experts that you see appearing regularly on cable and network shows do so without a publicist. They rely on the strategies outlined in this book coupled with old-fashioned tenacity. But there's always a way to improve your reach, strengthen your connections, and deepen your engagement.

When the producers or bookers are interested, they'll ask for your press kit. You're the one who provides the content for that, too.

Your Press Kit

A polished and professional press kit is the secret to opening doors. It lets bookers and producers know who you are, what you're about, and what you have to offer.

Most of the producers and bookers you'll be connecting with will say. "Can you send me a quick bio?" By *send* they mean "e-mail." By *bio* they mean "press kit." By *quick* they mean "NOW."

What goes in a press kit? Just three things: a short description of yourself (also known as a "one sheet"), a professional-quality photo, and a link to a video showing you in action. This is the kit you'll have ready to send along with your pitches. You may want to add other items, such as links to magazine or print features, lists of awards and accolades, or links to published articles and books. My recommendation is to have multiple versions of a press kit. They should vary in length and content and be specifically tailored for different audiences. The goal is to show your range, depth, and uniqueness—anything generic undermines your efforts.

Producers at this point will open an attachment (unlike the pitch stage). Avoid the rookie mistake of attaching a file that's so big no one can open it. Think short, small, and amazing!

One Sheet

This is what the producer needs to know about you. Keep it as simple as possible. Part of being a media-savvy expert is to talk in sound bites. Here's your chance to show the producers you can do that. Think of it as a very short résumé. Lead with a summary of your credentials, then list any appearances you've made. If you're just starting out, list anything else that's relevant—articles you've written, blog topics you've covered—whatever helps establish your expertise.

Every single person on TV today started out with a short one sheet they had to build on. Why should it be any different for you? When you look at your notes for the one sheet, what else would you like to see? If you think you're light on education in the field, sign up for online courses or workshops. If you'd like to list publications, but don't have any, hire a writer or write something yourself and publish it on Kindle.

Be honest with yourself. Make a point to fill in any blanks in your one sheet. Think strategically. Come up with manageable ways to add any training or experience you want to see as a part of your press kit.

Photo

Your photo needs to be the very best representation of you possible. If you haven't already been all over the media, your photo will be their first opportunity to get to know you. If you want to be in the big leagues, you have to present a professional appearance from the start. Invest $100 or so in a professional head shot. It will be worth it.

This photo needs to reflect your brand. So many people make the mistake of thinking they need a glam shot or that their head shot should look like the one they took for their high school yearbook. This is not about impressing your friends. It's about projecting your brand. Many of the professional head shots I have seen of Wolfgang Puck, for example, show him dressed in monogrammed chef's whites. This is strategic and smart. He looks like a famed chef whose name is synonymous with the culinary arts.

Puck could not have built three successful companies unless he was a skilled businessman, too, but if he wore a three-piece suit in his photos, it would not reinforce the culinary brand that sets him apart.

Video

Your press kit should also contain links to video clips of you speaking as an expert in your field. If you don't have clips, you can create an effective three-minute video at home. Find a topic to comment on, come up with three bullet points, and record yourself or have someone interview you on a topic. The key is making sure the video is high quality and the best representation of you.

When Samantha Schacher, who now appears regularly as a celebrity expert on CNN, HLN, MTV, CNBC, and Fox, was starting out, she didn't have any video for her press kit. "I wrote some faux segments to shoot, found a cameraman who could also edit them," she explained. "And boom! I had a reel."

Samantha did the footwork and slowly, but surely, began booking interviews. "Some were paid (very little), some were not, but I was gaining experience, connecting with industry people, finding my voice, finding my brand, and garnering more material—that is pivotal." As she built her reputation for having strong opinions and being well prepared, her need for pitching decreased. When stories broke, producers at media outlets wanted her reliable insights and began to seek her out.

Keep in mind the vast majority of stories and experts you see on TV were pitched! Most people assume that what they watch is on TV because it was so interesting that it deserved to be on air. It's not true. People are pitching producers with stories and offering to weigh in as experts. The producers go through the options and make their choices. Only occasionally, on breaking news stories where the clock is ticking and they haven't heard from enough experts, do they go looking.

The shared dream of executive producers, directors, hosts, and experts is that the story will take off and go viral. There's no reliable way to predict it. I've been a part of stories that started off small, then began popping up everywhere. Other broadcast stations started covering it, affiliates brought in commentators, the Associated Press picked it up, and newspapers sent reporters out to get interviews. When we Googled it, the stories were proliferating by the minute.

Responding with agility to unexpected boons like this is an essential part and parcel of a rainmaker's skill set. When you put together a solid pitch and press kit and do the work of putting yourself out there, you're making your own luck. When you're ready, the rewards can exceed anything you planned.

CHAPTER 5

Become a Trusted Source

We've talked about targets, pitches, and breaking news. Now let's talk about you.

What do you do *after* you get that call saying: "Wow, we loved your pitch! We looked at your video. You're great. We want you on our show!"? Getting the invitation is a great moment, but then you've got to deliver. Once you're sitting in front of the camera, how can you present your best self?

Ironically, coming across as your best, most authentic self is not always as easy as you'd think. We've all seen people get it wrong. Even the most accomplished actress, who has made us laugh, cry, and shout out loud in the movies, can come off awkward, stiff, and unnatural on TV.

Granted, playing a role on a set when someone else has written the lines requires very different skills from being your best self in the media. As I've said before, being an expert in the media is not acting. If you find yourself on *Good Morning America* or *The View* and you start *acting* like an expert, you'll never survive. Not only will the hosts and the producers cross you off their lists, but the audience will see through your act in a heartbeat!

It may be easier to put on an act, but it will never work on the air. The good news is, you don't have to fake it. I'm going to tell you exactly what you need to do to speak like a pro.

It starts with the critical branding information detailed in Chapter 2. As I've stated, knowing your brand is key. Clarity about your brand will give you an anchor for your comments and make your answers to any questions posed by the hosts or anchor easier to respond to. It will also help the audience to connect with you and the information you are conveying.

Psychotherapist Michael Dow knows that as long as he stays true to his brand of assessing every situation with an inquiry of how it impacts the heart and human behavior, it doesn't matter if he is providing expert opinions on *The Doctors* or the *Today* show, or hosting a cable show on weight loss, sex addiction, or breaking news. He is always looking for the relatable emotional component. Producers know what to expect and he consistently delivers.

As a result, he has expanded his brand further than he could've ever expected. Not only has his social media platform grown exponentially, but his regular appearances on shows like *Dr. Oz*, *Nightline*, *Access Hollywood Live*, and many others have allowed him to reach millions with his message. A higher profile has given him the opportunity to train some of the country's most respected doctors and host multiple cable TV shows. While many of his peers were helping others in quiet private practices, Michael Dow seized the opportunity to get his message out to millions more with media interviews. Because he did it well, producers were eager to have him back again and again.

The Rule of 4 will help ensure that you get invited back, too. Some people, like Dr. Dow, do it instinctively. Most of us have to learn these four golden rules and learn to put them into practice:

Rule 1: Point of View
Rule 2: Authenticity
Rule 3: Pivot
Rule 4: Sound Bite

You're going to need all four of these to succeed, and we'll take a look at each one. Master them and you'll be able to confidently express your own point of view with authority, get the audience on your side by being your authentic self, pivot with ease to the answers you want to give, and trim your message into sound bites that perfectly fit the time you have during most interviews.

Rule 1: Point of View

As an expert, you are not supposed to be neutral and objective. You have put in a lot of time, resources, and training to hone your craft, and no doubt along the way, you have formed strong opinions about the work that you do. As a law-enforcement expert, you may have formed opinions about why crime rates fluctuate, the best practices in policing, and how to train officers. Don't leave those opinions at the office when you are giving an interview with the media. You are not the anchor or the reporter; you are invited to express an informed opinion.

When I went on TV to talk about the sex assault criminal lawsuit filed against actor and comedian Bill Cosby, anchors always asked me: What did I think about the state's case? What did I think it meant for rape victims' rights and advocates? Did I think a conviction would impact pending civil lawsuits? Could I give my point of view on Cosby's statements about race as a factor in his prosecution? You'll always be asked for your opinion.

As an expert you are not reporting, you are commenting. When you watch the TV coverage of an event, they often show a video, or what is commonly referred to as a "package," then the anchor or host will summarize or reiterate what is played on tape. This is how they set up the story and lead into the segment where they bring in their expert.

Since the host has already recapped the video, you shouldn't do the same thing. You need to give the facts, but as an expert you should add more. Viewers are curious about how things

work. What's the backstory? How does all of this make any kind
of sense? What does it mean? How do you feel about what happened? What is your assessment of the event? They've already
seen what happened. They're hoping you'll help them interpret
the events and give them a frame from which to form their own
opinions.

By interpreting and analyzing what we saw, you help us
understand what we saw. Reporters and announcers give the
play-by-play. As an expert, you get to do the fun part: say what
you think about it!

When Dr. Dow was asked by the producers of *The Doctors* to
meet with a woman who was eating clay pots and to describe her
condition on air, it wasn't enough to simply state the facts about
how often she ate clay, what triggered her urge to eat the clay, and
the threats to her health from consuming the clay. They wanted
his opinion about what caused the behavior. After spending significant time meeting with her, he suggested that the origins of
her behavior may have originated in childhood. He believed that
unresolved issues—and not an iron deficiency—were likely to be
the main cause. Dr. Dow could have ended his analysis there, but
he went on to explain that most eating and compulsive disorders
are emotional, not physiological, issues.

The real question is: Do you know what you think? Have
you thought about the story through the lens of your brand? This
doesn't mean that every time you comment on a story, you have
the same response or reach the same conclusion. Though I frequently commented that I believed powerful men who are accused
of sexual assault are given a pass, I am also objective and willing to state that in some cases men are falsely accused, indicted,
and prosecuted. Having an opinion and a point of view is not
blind adherence to a position devoid of reality. Credibility always
matters.

Like everything else, the ability to form clear, succinct opinions that sound respectable can be improved with practice. Listen

to a news program with experts giving their opinions. What is your opinion on the matter? If you had to respond to their comments within seconds, what would you say? Could you limit your response to thirty seconds?

Challenge yourself. The next time you watch the news and see a story related to your area of expertise, formulate your opinion on the story. Think about how you would frame your response.

It's all about getting practice that's targeted to this very specific forum where you've got to answer quickly in a memorable, dynamic way.

You might have worked hard to improve your speaking skills. Lining up regular speaking engagements is an excellent way to build your following, but the skills do not necessarily cross over. Media appearances are fast and pithy. There's no time to give a long explanation full of overly technical terms, no matter how engaging it is. Learning to give your own authentic opinion in three minutes or less is a very specific skill.

- **Start Big.** Write down everything you'd like to say in an interview on a given topic. How many different points did you make? Which three talking points are most important to you?
- **Pare It Down to Three Minutes.** Whittle down the notes under those talking points until you have three minutes of material. People tend to speak at 150 to 200 words per minute. That means three minutes is usually about 500 words. But people talk at different speeds.
- **Time Yourself.** When you speak the text aloud, how long does it take you to read a page? Does your speaking rate speed up or slow down under pressure? Take advantage of the opportunity to videotape your response. Play it back and practice until you get better.
- **Build in Silence.** Dr. Phil McGraw once told me people tend to think that "more is more" when they're talking on TV. He emphasizes the importance of silence. If a host asks you

a question in a panel, you may need to answer quickly, but recognize that natural pauses can punctuate your words in a powerful way. People listen more when you say less, and your words are often more impactful. A well-placed pause can also help draw attention to your remarks on a show where other guests are aggressively competing for the mic.

Once you have developed your three-minute talking points, look for ways to sum up your talking points in a few pithy thirty-second sound bites. Sometimes a great sound bite may slip out of an expert's mouth while they're on the air. More likely than not, they have carefully crafted these sound bites ahead of time. You should do the same.

When I was asked if race was a factor in the Bill Cosby criminal sex assault case, I answered: "Race is always a factor in cases with African-American defendants." The quote went straight to social media. Quick, definitive statements are more likely to be heard and repeated.

Most people listening to your interview on a podcast or watching you on TV are multitasking. They're cooking dinner, helping kids with homework, or reading their texts. You rarely have a captive audience.

While they may remember what you've said for hours, they're most likely to repeat it or share it on social media if you sum up your message in a sound bite—something they can hashtag and quote on social.

Here's another example: When I was asked by a host to sum up the lawsuit we were discussing, I did not say, "Well, when two parties are in a conflict like this, the question becomes whether or not they actually entered into a contract. Was there an offer and an acceptance of that offer? Was there, in fact, a breach? And who caused said breach? Then we get to the issue of damages. The truth is, damages are very complicated—"

It's an answer a law professor might give, but TV listeners

aren't professors. They may want to hear what I have to say, but they're surrounded by distractions. I know that if I hope to break through the clutter and get their attention, I'll have to do it with a sound bite. So I smiled at the host and said: "No contract, no breach, no damages."

When you're developing your talking points, see how many of them can be conveyed in a sound bite, then memorize those key phrases. Think about what will stick in people's minds.

Rule 2: Authenticity

Be yourself on camera. When producers bring you on again and again, it's because they like your personality. They love it when you connect with their audiences. They want you—not someone posing as you or you pretending like you're someone else. Who are you? How much of yourself are you willing to reveal?

Authenticity does not mean you can't be polished and improved. It's just about making sure the real you shines through.

As a media-savvy expert, you are representing your brand. How do your interests, your values, your personality, and your message reflect the real you?

Before you start to present yourself as a commentator with a consistent brand, spend some time thinking about how you genuinely see the world. Like it or not, your comments are going to gravitate to your most natural point of view. Are you always outraged? Do you always see the good? Does it come more naturally to you to make cynical remarks, or are you invariably optimistic?

Put your strengths and weaknesses, your quirks, and your traits in the spotlight. Do a scan of your life, of all the experiences that matter to you most. If you were an outsider looking at the groups you belong to, the charities you serve, the music you like, what would it say to you?

The more you align your brand and presentation with your

true nature, the more sustainable, enjoyable, and natural it will be. So ask yourself: How can you make your brand the most authentic reflection of who you are?

Congresswoman Maxine Waters, who appears regularly on MSNBC, is known for her fireball, take-no-prisoners brand. She rose to prominence in the California state legislature in the 1970s in part because of the fearless manner in which she took on causes from calling on American companies to divest from South Africa to challenging local police departments on their record of racial profiling. Her brash and caustic language ignited her base, and thirty years later, that same aggressiveness has made her the darling of progressives.

Your brand and authenticity can't change with every appearance. You've got to align with your message until who you are becomes your brand. Fundamentally, people are who they are anyway, even when they try to be someone else. When Congresswoman Waters responded to a critique of her appearance by a Fox news anchor by saying, "I'm a strong black woman. You cannot intimidate me," no one doubted for a moment that she was being anything other than genuine.

If you try to be someone other than who you are, it's rarely successful. Once you sit down in front of the camera, people will feel it if you're not being yourself. We've got a sixth sense for fake.

In a recent appearance on HLN's *Primetime Justice with Ashleigh Banfield*, I stuck around after the show to talk with Ashleigh to get her feedback on my comments, as it was the first time that I was on set with her in New York. I asked Ashleigh if my presentation was what she expected, and if the substance and tone of my commentary fit with the style of her new show. I told her that I thought I could have been slightly more animated during some of the segments. She stopped me and reminded me that the reason she always liked having me on her show was because I conveyed a strong point of view without the histrionics that she said were displayed often by many commentators. I was pleased to get the positive feedback and affirmation of what I knew: being overly dramatic, loud, or disruptive is rarely valued by hosts. Find your voice and always use it. Leave the theatrics at home unless you find yourself on a late-night show or during carpool karaoke with a comedian.

The most successful people often have many different causes, products, and appearances, but at the core they're always themselves and they excel at conveying that. Earvin "Magic" Johnson has a big, gregarious personality. He's always been the cheerleader, the supporter, the leader. That's what he leverages in all the projects he does, whether he's building movie theaters, buying Starbucks, or becoming a partner in the Los Angeles Dodgers or the LA Lakers. No matter what's going on, he always brings that million-dollar Magic smile and an upbeat "we can do it" point of view. "Yes, this team is struggling," he may say, "but I have belief in these guys. We can turn this around."

Whoopi Goldberg is another great example of authenticity. She is always herself: a black woman, a skeptic, an outsider. She's an original who does things on her own terms, and that comes through whether she's talking about current events or promoting her latest show.

The message of my brand is advocacy but different people may deliver that message in very different ways. When I deliver that message, it takes my own traits. My personality comes through. I'm a Harvard lawyer using straight talk and tough love. I grew up in North St. Louis with everyday people, and although I am an Ivy League–trained attorney, at the heart of it, my deep Midwestern and urban roots are very much a part of who I am. Like Dr. Travis says, you're not going to yell me down, because I do my homework, I am prepared, and I will stand up for a position I believe in. I've always been that way. All you have to do is watch me on TV to see that these traits are authentic. You'd know it if they weren't.

I'm also a passionate advocate for kids and families. You can't

fake that, either. You can't pretend to care about kids and families.
It will be reflected in what you say and what you do. I wouldn't
just line up a few photo ops with children in need and call myself
an advocate. I've got to get in there, do the work, stay involved,
and try to make a real difference.

Over time, as I began to establish myself, I found new opportunities to bring more traits and interests under the rubric of my
brand. That's one reason I love working on daytime talk shows
like *Dr. Phil* and *The Doctors*. Daytime shows allow me to be
witty—to indulge my love of fashion, to show my sense of humor
and my lighter side. When I show up at night to talk about police
shootings on CNN, there is nothing light about it, no jokes to be
had. But as long as it's authentically who you are, and appropriate
to the tone of the show, variety can be good for your brand.

Rule 3: Pivot

When the wrong winner of the Best Picture was announced at
the Oscars in 2017, the unprecedented blunder instantly became
the top story in entertainment news. It was all anyone could talk
about for the next twenty-four hours. The good news for director
Barry Jenkins was that his winning movie, *Moonlight*, will never
be forgotten. The bad news was, the story of the mix-up threat-
ened to completely overshadow the win.

The first thing every interviewer wanted him to do was comment on the blunder. Jenkins acknowledged the questions and
answered them briefly, graciously trying to keep the emphasis off
of the embarrassing mistake. ("I love *La La Land* . . . how can you
not?") And then he proved he was a pro with a beautiful pivot:
"It's unfortunate that things happened the way they did, but—*hot
damn!*—we won Best Picture!"[1]

No matter how well prepared you are, you will inevitably be
asked questions from time to time that you don't want to answer or
don't know the answer to. In some situations, you will simply have

to admit that you don't know the answer, you lack sufficient information, or you are waiting to form an opinion until you receive additional facts. In other situations, you can pivot—that is, give an answer that is not exactly responsive to the question, but conveys your key message. When you succeed, it not only demonstrates your expertise, it allows you to shift your answer toward the area where you can add the most value.

This is routinely done in media interviews. The key is to do it in a way that doesn't offend your host. If you have ever watched Don Lemon on *CNN Tonight*, you have probably seen him end interviews with guests who have refused to answer questions. This can be humiliating and embarrassing, but it is easily avoided by always answering the host's questions.

The key is to control the focus. Often in interviews, you have a point you want to make. The reason you're on the air is to spread the word about something. You want to convey your message. Interviewers may be happy to let that happen, but they have a different agenda. They are not necessarily going to ask you the perfect question to set up your message. Most likely, you'll get to answer two questions—at most, three or four. The odds are good that you will never be asked the question you deem to be the "right" question. Getting your message across is on you.

When you appear as a guest expert, you are entering into a conversation with the host and other guests. Once you're on the air, you may find the host pulling the story in a direction that takes it away from your message and the talking points you developed. As in any conversation, you can't always anticipate what will happen, but you can do a few things to reduce the odds of being taken by surprise.

- **Know the Habits of Your Host.** I've said it before, but by watching the host beforehand, you can learn a lot about what kind of questions they ask, how much time they allow guests to respond, and what cues they give before they change the subject. If you do your homework, you will have an advantage in steering the conversation back to your message if necessary.

- **Be Ready to Pivot.** If the conversation turns toward a point of view that you disagree with, pivot back to your position and present your expert opinion in a nonhostile way. Go back to your talking points. Remember, you're not going to change the mind of the host or the guests when you're arguing different opinions. Judge your success instead by how well you've articulated your own points for listeners.

- **Study the Pros.** Part of learning any new skill is paying careful attention to those who already do it well. Notice how often professionals take charge of the conversation and lead it back to the points they want to make. Make notes about the transitions they use to get back on point. Practice your favorite lines until you are confident you'll be able to wield them under pressure.

In every field in every country, those with the most experience in doing interviews have learned how to pivot. Some do it so seamlessly, viewers don't even notice they've changed the subject.

After British prime minister Theresa May lost the support she was hoping for from a vote in 2017, an interviewer asked her a brutal question: "Don't you think you ought to resign?" Whatever her failings may be, May is highly experienced at giving interviews. Her eyes didn't even flicker. She simply pivoted to her message: "The important thing is that we continue to strengthen our communication with Europe throughout this Brexit process."

It's a skill that can be earned with preparation and practice.

In recent years, I've appeared as a legal expert on MSNBC or CNN to talk about the rise of social justice movements like Black Lives Matter and attacks on police in Dallas, New York, and other cities. On July 7, 2016, I was booked on *CNN Tonight* to discuss the police shootings of Philando Castile in Minnesota and Alton Sterling in Louisiana, which had happened earlier in the week. In the midst of the broadcast, host Don Lemon was notified that five Dallas police officers were killed and twelve shot by a sniper at the end of a scheduled rally to protest the killing of Castile and Sterling. This devastating news resulted in the show being extended for two hours.

As Don Lemon, the other panelists, and I tried to make sense of the attacks on the officers and provide up-to-the-minute coverage and analysis of the brutal police attack, I had to ensure that my commentary reflected the sincere sorrow and dismay that I felt. I, like the rest of the panel, was heartbroken over the news that officers were killed in the line of duty and thousands of innocent protestors' lives were placed in jeopardy. Because of the outspoken position I had taken on the spate of African-American men who had been shot and the ensuing protests, it was also important to constantly remind the audience that similar protests were peaceful and resist those who wanted to make a correlation between the lone shooter and the protests that involved thousands and had had no reports of violence.

Even in difficult situations, as a professional and a brand, your voice should be consistent. While condemning the violent act of the shooter, it was important to emphasize the impact and importance of peaceful protests. Throughout the four hours of live coverage of the police shooting, my commentary continued to include expressions of sorrow for the officers and factual information on how peaceful protests were often being negatively characterized and that they were responsible for the prolonged media coverage and, in part, the changes within police departments around the country.

I knew that marches had been instrumental in changing policies that required policemen to wear body cameras, to provide information to the public about the shooters, and to determine more quickly if the district attorney was going to file charges. Yet the news coverage of protests often focused on random violence or looked for ways to sensationalize the story. To me, it was important to show that protests were moving the needle. Legislators were taking notice, reconsidering their positions on the issues, and taking action as a result.

Whenever I appeared on shows on the topic of police shootings, I had to find a way to bring that into the story. Because the hosts had footage of police brutality, the questions they asked were: "What do you make of this video tape? To the layperson, this may look like excessive force on the part of the policeman, but what's the legal standard?"

First, I always answered the question: "Yes, this does seem to demonstrate excessive force. He was shot in the back. So many other de-escalation tactics could've been used instead."

Whenever I could, I added, "It's also important to mention that a lot of these instances of police violence are getting attention because of protests. These cases aren't new. Video recording on cell phones is new. Live-streaming it is new. But the multiethnic protests and outrage we're seeing in New York, Los Angeles, and Chicago have been happening all along. The difference is, they're having a much bigger impact now than ever before, because people around the world can see instantly what's going on."

As a civil rights attorney, I would always be interested in a case about police brutality. But if I'm on the air, I want to not only share my legal expertise but also get my message out: Advocacy matters. It makes a real difference. Pivoting allows me to do that.

The same thing happens when I am interviewing a guest on *The Doctors* about a botched plastic surgery. My first comment is always along these lines:

> "Thank you for having the courage to share your story. By doing so, you are empowering other women to speak out and in doing so helping to improve the level of medical care for all women."

Remember, advocacy is my brand, so I consciously connect the story to it.

If you don't know your message or you don't find a way to work it in, it won't happen. It would be random luck if a host happened to ask my opinion on the effectiveness of public protests when they have a viral videotape about police brutality. You've got to pivot.

Rule 4: Sound Bite

No matter how much you have to say, you have to do it in sound bites. You can't make your point three and a half minutes into the interview if you've got only three minutes. Do the math.

If you're working hard to be the go-to expert in your niche, you've obviously got a lot of information to share. It's not about that. It's about being savvy enough to understand the limits and professional enough to hit your mark within those limits.

It's not uncommon for me to spend three hours preparing for a three-minute interview—in addition to the time I spend staying on top of the issues. After I've done my research, I could make important points on the subject for hours, but I don't have hours and the audience doesn't, either. I have disciplined myself to step back from all the information I've garnered and make my choices. I know I'll have time to make three, maybe four, points at most. If the direction of the conversation shifts, I may not even get to do that. So I've got to choose wisely.

This isn't a competition or a high school debate. Nor are you going to score points by being the person who talks the most, uses the most polysyllabic words, overtalks the host, or gives long, convoluted answers that cause you to lose your audience and irritate your host and other guests.

A good sound bite relies on brevity and pacing. If you talk too fast, people won't understand you. If you talk too slow, you will bore the audience and lose valuable time for more questions.

It's hit and run. You get in, make the points that advance the conversation most, and get out. The hope is that people who are interested in hearing more will either seek you out or keep watching the coverage of the issue to stay informed. You're there to say a few words that pique their interest and bullet-point the most important things they need to know. Many times, a show producer will post any poignant and cogent responses you make to a host's question on social media. They oftentimes will even post the actual clip of the back-and-forth with you and the host. CNN frequently does this. During the 2016 U.S. presidential election, it was routine to see clips highlighting political analysts Van Jones, Ana Navarro, and others. Having your segment amplified thousands of times over is motivation enough to follow this rule.

It comes back again to the question: "Why does this matter?" That's what you're there to let them know.

A politician who claims to support human rights lies about his financial links to a man whose name most people have never heard before. Why does it matter? With your talking points ready, you tell people exactly why: This mystery man is a criminal involved in human trafficking around the world. The politician is a hypocrite who says one thing and does another—at the cost of human lives.

A new study reveals that oversight on food labeling is surprisingly lax. Why does it really matter? Because there's a disturbing increase in produce being mislabeled "organic" when, in fact, it's genetically modified food that's been treated with toxic pesticides, you explain.

In both cases, you undoubtedly have a lot more interesting things to say. Maybe that politician has a lurid history of associating with the underworld and you know all the details. Or your research has shown that, in fact, not all genuinely "organic" produce rises to the same standard. But the chances are you won't have time to go into all that. Take your three-minute window and make the most of it.

It's challenging at first, but believe me, it gets better with experience. Eventually, the option of speaking in super-concise sound bites starts to actually feel natural. You can do this.

One way to start building on your experience is to look at an interview with an expert in your niche on a show you want to pitch.

Suppose you are a geologist in the business of assessing the impact of climate change. You see on YouTube that in February 2017, Tucker Carlson interviewed Bill Nye, the Science Guy, about climate change on Fox News for nine minutes and twenty-two seconds.[2]

As you watch the interview, write down the questions that Tucker Carlson asks. Think about what your own answers would be and jot them down. Then play the interview again, hitting the Mute button whenever Bill Nye speaks. That's when you speak instead.

Keep in mind that you don't have any more time to answer than Bill Nye did. If Tucker Carlson cuts him off, he cuts you off, too. Deal with it.

You can do the same thing spontaneously when you watch the news at night. Hit Mute when the expert speaks and stop talking when they stop. Better yet, record yourself being interviewed by the anchors. We've got the technology. You can practice a virtual interview with the actual segment. Whether you record it with a camera or not, the exercise will give you practice in keeping your answers short while getting in your talking points.

The more practice you get, the better you'll refine your skills at getting your message across in cogent sound bites.

Seize the Moment

It always amazes me when some of my favorite actors go onstage to accept awards at the Oscars and, as excited as I am about their win, I tune out what they're saying within minutes.

"This is unbelievable! When I was a small child in Georgia..."

Zzzzz!

"Thank you, thank you! I'd like to thank the director, the

executive producer, the second unit director, the line producer, the camera operator, the caterer..." *Zzzzzz!*

You've only got a few minutes under the spotlight. Plan ahead and make it great.

Anderson Cooper 360° is broadcast live from CNN's Time Warner Center studios in New York. Every second of airtime is precious. When I go on as legal analyst, I might have time to say, "Hi Anderson, it's good to see you again." Or if I'm asked a question right away, I might just leave it at "Hi, Anderson" and cut to the chase. A lot of experts don't even say "Hi."

It's not a social call. You don't have to worry about appearing rude or hurting anyone's feelings. Everybody in the studio—the director, the producers, and Anderson himself—is focused on grabbing the attention of the audience. So squeeze in a quick "Hi" if you can, then make sure the first statement out of your mouth is catchy. If you say something generic ("Can you believe this horrible crime, Anderson?"), you'll lose the audience.

Ideally, you will find a way to lead with your own message. In his first interview after the State of the Union in 2014, President Obama gave a perfect example of that.

CNN's Jake Tapper asked, "How much can you really accomplish [with executive orders]?"

Obama pivoted immediately to a topic of greater interest to more of his audience and, at the same time, linked it to his own optimistic brand: "Well, first of all, my big push is making sure we're focused on opportunity."

As I write this, you can still find that interview on CNN's channel on YouTube.[3] Whether it's still there or not, YouTube is a great place to look for examples of opening lines. You can learn almost as much from the lines that put you to sleep as you can from the lines that make you eager to hear what else the expert has to say.

You can do a generic search for "news interviews" or, if you already know which shows are the best fit for your brand, narrow the field accordingly: "CNN interviews," "Dr. Oz interviews," "Stephen Colbert interviews."

It's a good way to become an expert in opening lines. While you're at it, identify the experts' talking points. How many did they manage to get in? Can you tell when the topic changes and they have to quickly shift gears? Notice their timing, pacing, and body language, too. How are they dressed? How much or little do they use their hands?

Listen Under Duress

Whether you appear as an expert in a radio studio with a single host or on TV with two hosts and three more experts, the pressure will be on. This is the time to take your listening skills to a new level.

You've got to be thinking about your own appearance: "How can I get in my talking points? Have I conveyed my message well enough yet?" At the same time, you've got to be in the moment, listening carefully to what the host and the other guests are saying.

Some guests may be in the studio with the host while others are in another city, sitting in front of a green screen that the production team will replace with an image of an urban landscape. The host will be talking to all of you at once.

You've got to listen very carefully to what's being said to know when it's your turn and be thinking about how you can add something new to advance the conversation. Can you imagine what it would feel like to make a comment only to have the other expert tell you, "That's what I just said"?

Because you're under pressure and have a lot on your mind, you need to learn how to listen with a lot of other things going on, while thinking carefully about the next thing you're going to say. It's multitasking under pressure.

Some people can do this naturally. If you're not one of them, take the time to practice. One way to do that is to turn on the TV news and the radio at the same time and listen to what the anchor is saying. Imagine how you'd answer her questions, if you were on the air. Any time you find the opportunity to think of several things at once while listening carefully to other people, do it. It can only improve your skill.

Know the Other Guests

Even if you think you know who they are already, it never hurts to Google the host and the other guests you'll be appearing with. If the producer does not tell you who else will be on the show with you, be sure to ask. Knowing who they are and where they're coming from ahead of time can give you an edge.

If you know another guest consistently holds an opposing opinion, you'll be able to keep certain rebuttals in mind. If you're not up-to-date on their opinions, you can miss a beat. Take it from me. I recently appeared with an expert I thought I knew. Because of the impression I had of him, I made certain assumptions about his opinions. When we got on the air, his point of view was literally the opposite of what I'd expected. So it threw me for a loop.

Don't let that happen to you. It takes minutes to Google the host and other guests. Seek out their opinions. Look for articles they've written. Find something that tells you what they're likely to say. Knowing where they're coming from will help you form your own talking points to advance the conversation. You need facts and the latest information to do that.

The background research you do rightfully reinforces the impression that you are up on what's happening, the best informed person in the room. "I was watching Dan Green the other day and he made this same point without any facts to support it," you might say on the air. "Today he's making that same point again, but there are still no facts to support it."

Get the Names Right

This is one of those things that seems obvious, yet a lot of people don't do it.

First of all, before you go on the show, ask the producer who will conduct the interview (unless it is a show with only one host) and who the other guests will be. Look up their photos. Read their bios. And most of all, know their names. Learn and remember the name of the producer who invited you on the show, too.

While you're completing your preparation, be sure to look up the pronunciations of all the proper names that might come up—not only of the hosts, but also the celebrities, politicians, organizations, and countries—while you're on the air.

In private conversation, your friends may shrug and laughingly admit they don't know how to pronounce a tricky name, either, but as an expert speaking to millions of viewers you're expected to take the lead. If you don't know, who does?

Check out all the names related to the discussions. Names move very quickly once you're on the air. You don't want to be hearing an unfamiliar name for the first time. Be prepared.

It's hard to sound like an expert in international relations if you clumsily pronounce *Iraq* like "eye rack" or stumble over "Abu al-Khayr al-Masri" when you comment on his death in a drone strike.

Celebrity experts face similar challenges. In 2014, when *12 Years a Slave* became the first film directed and produced by a black filmmaker to win an Oscar, director Steve McQueen's name was easy enough to pronounce. The names got more challenging when Chiwetel Ejiofor won best actor and Lupita Nyong'o won best actress.

Getting a name wrong is a surefire way to create doubt about your substantive knowledge. After all, audiences are expecting experts to be a cut above! Not only do you lose credibility as an expert and a professional if you get a name wrong, but you open yourself up for attack.

I've had people call me the wrong name on the air. Normally, I let it go. But if they cross the line, I will call them out. One particularly obnoxious expert on a show talked over me every time I said anything. To make matters worse, his research was sloppy. He kept citing "facts" that I knew to be wrong or outdated. Every time I called him on it, he dug in harder. It was starting to turn into a battle, and then he made a mistake, fumbling my name. In a voice dripping with condescension, he said, "Well, that's where you're wrong, Reva—" I interrupted him and easily put him in his place, since all I had to say was: "First of all, my name is Areva...."

Be Cooperative, Not Combative

Remember you are there to participate in the conversation. If you are combative, unprepared, badly informed, don't answer questions, or alienate the host, you are creating enemies instead of colleagues who look forward to having you back on the show. You have to abide by the rules of the show. It's their house. Respect that.

Being combative is different from having a strong opinion. After an episode of *The Doctors*, Dr. Travis Stork came up to me shaking his head and said something like, "Boy, Areva, when you form an opinion, there's no convincing you otherwise. You stay with it tenaciously." And he's right. That's very different from being so rude and uncooperative to a host or the producers that they have to cut you off!,

Sometimes a producer will approach me before the show and set new limits. "We know that some outlets are saying that the police found the gun in this shooting, but we haven't been able to substantiate that. So please don't mention it. If it comes up, just say it's been reported, but not substantiated." This happens a lot, especially on MSNBC, CNN, and other news sites with reputations for journalistic integrity.

Even when a topic I was hoping to discuss is restricted, I naturally respect their guidelines. A producer might say, "Protests about this shooting are all over the news, but I'd rather stay focused on police brutality itself for this segment." As much as I'd like to, I'd be foolish to go back to my theme of protests in that situation. It's their show. You can't come in and hijack it.

Dogged interviewers will not let it go if you are combative, refuse to answer a question, or otherwise break the rules of engagement. If you cross them, any good host is fully capable of saying, "OK, let's move on to the next guest." A few of them will cut your microphone off!

In a 2017 segment on CNN about the high travel expenses of the first family, Don Lemon was interviewing a panel of four expert guests when Paris Dennard, a political pundit, tried to shut down the premise of the story. Even though he'd been asked to speak on the topic, he opened by stonewalling: "I think this is fake news."

The other guests laughed. Don Lemon said, "OK, Paris, hold on.... Do you actually know what the definition of 'fake news' is?"

"What we're doing right now," Dennard said.

"Fake news is when you put out a story to intentionally deceive someone and you know that it is wrong," Lemon explained. He added, "This story that we're doing right now is not [meant] to intentionally deceive anyone. We're simply talking about the cost to keep a president safe... There is nothing fake about that.

"Please stop it with that stupid talking point that it is a fake news story. If you don't want to participate in the news stories on this network, then don't come on and participate. But don't call them fake because you don't agree with them. Go on."

Refusing to join the discussion and flatly ignoring what Lemon had said, Dennard deafly repeated himself: "Don, this is a fake news story—"

But Lemon cut him off. "OK.... Thanks, everyone, for watching. Have a great weekend."[4]

People talk over each other 50 to 60 percent of the time on these shows. Rude guests appear maybe 20 percent of the time. So eventually, you will run into an obnoxious guest. If the show loves sparring between the guests, that's fine. But most shows don't like it. Again, you've got to know the show you're on.

In case you do find yourself on the air with an obnoxious guest, here are a few tips:

- **Remain Professional.** Remember you're a guest of the show. You've been invited. Respect that. Conduct yourself accordingly. People are invited on to make the show better. Make good TV for the network. If you don't do that, you won't be invited back.
- **No Overtalk.** Most shows will say, "Don't talk over each other. If you do, no one can hear anyone!" On *Dr. Drew*, the producer was always telling us, "You have to talk individually. Otherwise, it's just noise!" Even shows that want you to be aggressive and take conflicting positions don't want you to talk over each other so no one can hear either one of you. Wait. Let them make their point and jump in when you can.
- **Get Help.** Ideally, the host will intervene, but some hosts are bad at controlling the conversation. If the guest doesn't shut up, address the host by name and say, "Can you ask your guest to allow me to finish my comment?" or "I'd like to finish my comment." Even a reluctant host will take the nudge and then tell their guest, "You've had your turn. Let her speak."
- **No Name-Calling.** If the other person gets down in the mud and starts calling you names or saying you're a liar and making it personal, obviously you should resist any urge

to reciprocate. The best way to make a statement is not to stoop to their level. The guest may not notice, but the host, producers, and viewers will.

Consistently Add Value

When I studied public speaking, I was taught to tell stories, the more personal the better. People like stories and appreciate the opportunity to get to know you by having a little more insight into who you are. When you tell your own story, you can be highly authentic and infuse it with your own emotions. People sense how meaningful it is to you and feel a connection. You may even say something that really resonates with them.

As an expert that is media savvy, you're trying to make a connection, just as you do in public speaking. But telling a story takes time you usually don't have, and you need them to trust you quickly.

Believe it or not, research can get you part of the way there. Let's take the example of the Oscar blunder again. Suppose the viewers turned to the show to find out more about what happened. The host sets it up: "This was the biggest mishap in Oscar history."

Viewers are happy to watch the host play the video again showing the chaos on stage after Faye Dunaway said *La La Land* had won Best Picture, not realizing she was looking at the card for Best Actress. The host explains what the story is about, and then brings in the expert. "Joining me tonight is our entertainment correspondent. Hi, Jaylee. What are we to make of last night?"

What a media expert is supposed to do at that point is add new insights: "This has never happened in the eighty-three years PricewaterhouseCoopers has been running the Oscars, Rick. As you know, PricewaterhouseCoopers is the international accounting firm hired to..." Sadly, that doesn't always happen. All too often, they mistakenly believe that they're reporters and simply regurgitate the same information again: "Well, as we saw, Rick, there was a lot of confusion on stage—"

In their eagerness to hear more, suppose the viewers don't even notice that the entertainment correspondent, Jaylee, just repeated what they'd already heard. Maybe they were looking at her dress or thinking how much they liked her hair and not really listening. But if the minutes start ticking by and nobody adds new insights, those viewers are going to change stations with a flick of the remote.

The Oscar story was filled with opportunities for an expert to bring fascinating information that answers viewers' questions and puts the story in context. Why has PricewaterhouseCoopers been running the Oscars for eighty-three years? What do they even do? Why does it take a high-end accounting firm to tally the votes? What was the protocol for handing out the cards, and how did it go so wrong? Should they be hired for the next year's Oscars?

Answering those questions gives you an interesting angle supported by facts that set you apart. It can get you on a show and make your appearance memorable once you're there.

If you do that every time you appear, people start remembering it. They tune in when they hear you're going to be on. They stay to listen because they want to know what you have to say. "She always adds something great." "I always learn something new from her." "I love her point of view and rely on her opinions to help me understand complex issues." They tell their friends. They come to rely on that. They trust you. That's what you want because then you're more than just the go-to media expert.

You're a trusted source.

PART III

DEPLOY IT

CHAPTER 6

Go for Media Channels—Big and Small

I t's always tempting to reach for the biggest, shiniest brass ring. No matter how many major TV shows I do—even when I cohost an Emmy-winning syndicated talk show, *The Doctors*— people still say to me, "When are you going to have your own show?" "Why don't you go on this show or that?" Nothing you ever do is enough.

In our competitive, aspirational society, it's easy to get caught up in the constant striving to go bigger and do more. You have to keep your wits about you and resist those urges. You're not going to be able to do everything. Whatever other people may think, there's no need to do it all.

Mark Ridley-Thomas, chairman of the Board of Supervisors in the Second District of Los Angeles, is a perfect example. With an operating budget of more than $30 billion, LA County is the largest municipal government in the country.[1]

When Ridley-Thomas got elected it was not only the first time the board had elected an African-American man, it was the same year that Barack Obama was elected as the first African-American president. As the frenzy for African-American leadership started to build, invitations poured in. Soon Ridley-Thomas was being invited to give speeches and participate in forums in Washington, D.C., New York, and other big cities around the world. From the moment he took office, people were putting pressure on him to leverage his position and make himself a national figure.

As tempting as it surely must have been, Ridley-Thomas resisted that impulse because of his innate desire and connection to his goal to serve the people who elected him. He started turning down the shiny invitations to appear in the most coveted venues. Instead he drove his focus deep into the issues related exclusively to LA County. With a population of 10 million people, the county is larger than Sweden.[2] It's GDP of $930 billion makes it one of the largest economies in the world.[3] Ridley-Thomas quickly became one of the most powerful elected officials in California.

No doubt he could have leveraged that power for his own career from the start, but by devoting himself to LA County, he was able to insure that an underserved community of the poor, the homeless, the sick, and the marginalized got better services. He led hundreds of civic leaders, residents, health care advocates, and business owners in rebuilding the Martin Luther King, Jr. Community Hospital, which had been closed for nearly ten years.[4] In 2017, he led the way in passing a ballot initiative, Measure H, to add about $355 million annually for homeless programs.

Focusing on local concerns, instead of giving in to the impulse to go national, has made all the difference. Not only has he been effective in getting major initiatives passed, but he's built a reputation as a government official who can successfully take a project from start to finish. He's put programs into effect that have become models for other states. They all have the potential to make a national impact, but he couldn't have done it unless his focus had stayed local.

With your business, sometimes the best alignment for your brand will be a podcast or live stream with a perfectly targeted audience, instead of a national network with famous hosts that pleases you personally and impresses your friends, but reaches such a broad audience that it actually has less impact on growing your brand.

Always keep your brand in mind. Know your audience. Focus on your message. Never lose sight of your goal. As you evaluate the available media channels and make decisions about which shows to start pitching, take the time to think more deeply how you can convey your message in these venues.

Bigger Isn't Always Better

Most media experts are folks like me. We didn't leave an influential job at the White House and start appearing on major news show the next day. We had to work for it, building brick by brick, keeping a tight hold on our confidence and belief in our dreams even on the days when it didn't look like it was happening. Just so you know, if you have to work hard and be persistent, even when your pitches are met with rejection or silence over and over again, you're on the right track. Don't give up. That's the story of most successful people you see in the media.

Now I'm on CNN, *Good Morning America*, *Dr. Phil*, and *The Doctors*, but after getting that lucky break on the *Dr. Phil* show, when business started pouring in and I realized I wanted to do more, I worked hard to build my reel with appearances on local TV and web-based programs.

Never imagine that local markets are a waste of your time. Very few people shoot to a national platform overnight. If that's your target, it's definitely attainable. You'll learn how to leverage local appearances into national appearances by persistently getting the attention of producers on national programs. But the key is knowing where your people are and what's best for you, your brand, and business. Your success on year two should not be measured by someone else's twenty years in the field. There is simply no comparison.

What's important to realize is that bigger isn't always better. Suppose you're an expert in landscaping in Atlanta and you make an appearance on an HGTV show on cable to talk about gardening tips that will result in a beautiful lawn all year long. HGTV has more than 95 million viewers—more viewers than CNN. It's the third most watched cable channel in the United States after Fox News and ESPN.[5]

It's an exciting opportunity and, unless you're crazy busy, you should never turn it down. At the very least, it's a wonderful opportunity to generate name recognition, add a high-quality clip to your reel, make connections at HGTV that will be invaluable for many years to come, and build your social media following, if you amplify it the way I'll teach you in Part IV. But despite all that, it may not be the ideal venue.

If your primary goal is to increase your revenue, an appearance at a local station may be much more effective. Think about it. Your odds of returning after the show to a stack of phone messages are undoubtedly much greater if you appear on a high-profile show with millions of viewers. But if you want to work exclusively in Atlanta and your callers want to hire you for landscaping in Seattle, Austin, Baltimore, and Denver, the show didn't reach your target audience.

Suppose you're a chef with an expertise in Spanish cuisine. At your new restaurant in Rancho Palos Verdes, California, you've created an inkfish paella that is getting stellar reviews. The line outside your door winds around the corner on Friday nights. If you decide to run a special on Wednesdays to bring people in midweek, you don't let everyone in Pasadena, California, know about it. Your people are in Rancho Palos Verdes.

My friend, Anahita Sedaghatfar, Esq., is one of those rare people who was actually "discovered" like a starlet in the Golden Age of Hollywood. After she argued a contentious motion in a packed courtroom in LA, a stranger offered to put her in touch with a friend who was a producer on Fox News. In Los Angeles everyone claims to be somebody, so she told him she wasn't interested. But the next day she got a call from the Fox News producer in New York. She ended up on a major network on her first TV show the same week.

"I was so nervous," Anahita said, "because I had never appeared on television before and now, suddenly, I was going on a national news network. No one gave me any kind of training, tips, or help. I really had no idea what to expect.

"I did the segment and surprisingly, it felt so natural to me. I was hooked. After that one segment, I started to get calls and e-mails from many producers on Fox News, Fox Business Channel, CNN, and HLN. I haven't stopped since."

Curiously enough, Anahita moved to local news stations after the national ones. After a few months, she found that appearing on local networks expanded her law practice significantly—even more so than national appearances.

Not only are local markets a better match for certain business models, but there is far less competition. The doors are more likely to open, you're more likely to be met with favor, and they're more likely opportunities for long-standing relationships. You may consider them a starting point or an end goal. Either way, local markets should never be neglected.

Media Channels

Although your brand, your audience, and your message stay the same, your goals for specific media channels can vary. Sometimes you may appear on a show to create more brand recognition. Other times you will focus on driving traffic to your site or making sales.

Once you've selected the shows and channels that suit your brand, diversify within those choices. It's the same sensible approach you'd use with a stock portfolio. No financial investor would advise you to invest only in one company or industry. A healthier, more secure portfolio includes a range of investments. The same principle applies to media channels.

It will be up to you to decide which ones qualify to meet the needs of your brand. Let's take a look at a selection of channels where you're likely to get a live interview, starting with the newest options first.

Live Streams on Digital Channels

In 2016 Facebook launched a new publishing feature called Facebook Live. It is a huge opportunity to generate traction on social media by streaming live videos to your page. We will talk more about how to use it to your advantage on social media in Chapters 8 and 9.

News networks have been quick to adopt live streams on digital channels to augment and build momentum for the regularly scheduled shows they broadcast. I've flown to New York for NBC to do a stand-alone Facebook Live interview for NBCBLK, without doing an accompanying interview on any other MSNBC or NBC show.

Live streaming attracts so much attention that all the outlets are trying to incorporate it as quickly as possible to catch up. It's good news for guest experts, since it literally doubles or triples the number of venues we can appear in.

When the media outlet has both a TV and live-stream component, like Essence.com, you can pitch them separately. The pitch and talking points are the same. Only the venue is different. These online verticals are so new that there is not yet a good way to search for live stream segments and track down their producers. The best approach is to closely follow the shows you want to appear on and notice whether they've started using live streams or not and how often. If they do, you can call the show and find out who to contact about pitching your appearance on upcoming streams.

Some outlets, like *Good Morning America*, tend to combine a regularly scheduled show and a stream. I've appeared on a segment of the morning show, then stayed to answer questions on the same topic from a digital reporter who was live streaming our interview.

CNN was the first network to stream twenty-four-hour news online and on mobile.[6] In 2016, ABC News made a deal with Facebook to live stream the U.S. presidential debates and its predebate series *Straight Talk* on Facebook Live. The predebate allowed ABC to capture the attention of millennials before the debates started. As the stream ended, digital host Amna Nawaz told viewers she was going to *Nightline* to continue the conversation with coanchor Dan Harris and ABC News expert contributor LZ Granderson. *Nightline* literally picked up where the live stream left off, bringing a lot of new viewers to the show.

When ABC ran a live stream of the Democratic and Republican National Conventions on Facebook earlier in the year, it had gone so well, they wanted to do it again. That feed had brought more than 28 million video views to ABC's Facebook Pages.[7]

For the debate, ABC was starting to see the possibilities more clearly. This time, when they broadcast the live video on Facebook, they improved the level of engagement. They actively interacted with the audience and incorporated viewers' comments and questions in the Facebook Live coverage of the debates. As a sign that they really did understand the unprecedented value these streams were adding to their brand, ABC did not include any advertising in the feeds.[8]

Eager to catch up with the live-streaming trend already taking place on Twitter, Periscope, YouTube, and Snapchat, Facebook invested $50 million on live video deals with 140 celebrities and companies, such as the Metropolitan Museum of Art, the Museum of Natural History in New York, the FC Barcelona sports team, DJs Armin van Buuren and Hardwell, along with Internet celebrities like Logan Paul, Andrew Bachelor, and Lele Pons.

In one of the deals, Facebook spent $1 million for Tastemade, a foodie video network, to produce 100 Facebook Live shows a month for a year.[9] One Facebook Live video streamed by Buzz-Feed in connection with its Facebook deal brought in 10.8 million viewers. In the video a rubber band was stretched around a watermelon. After forty-five minutes, it exploded.[10]

Every time a publisher streams a video live, Facebook sends a notification to their fans. The strategy to promote Facebook Live has changed interactions on social media. In January 2016, only 11 percent of the top 500 Facebook Pages of media companies produced live videos. By May, 44 percent were posting live videos. Facebook users now watch 100 million hours of video in their feeds every day. Since Facebook stores the live streams, more than 65 percent of them watch it after it has aired.[11]

As Steven Perlberg and Deepa Seetharaman reported for the *Wall Street Journal*, "Chief Executive Mark Zuckerberg is betting that live videos will provide a further lift in user engagement, getting people to come to the service more often and stay longer."[12] There is every reason to believe he's right.

The major networks are already starting to incorporate it into their programming. After I appeared for a three-minute spot as an expert on the Fox LA affiliate last year, anchor Christine Devine asked me to stay for a Facebook Live interview to cover the issues in more depth after the show. We sat down together in a studio and talked for over an hour!

The Facebook Live feed went directly to the Fox Facebook page, but because of the stored streams, I was able to post it to my own page later, too. When a Facebook page has more followers than the broadcast, you may literally have more people watching your live stream than you'd have on the show itself!

A publicist told me that shows like *Access Hollywood* and *Dr. Oz* now specifically book her clients on Facebook Live segments. They are always longer—thirty to forty-five minutes instead of the usual three- to five-minute slots on the air. On Facebook, you have to allow time for people to populate the segment and come online.

Another major difference that's a real boon to rainmaking is that online streaming allows the audience to type in questions on the spot. So it's never an interview between the host and guest alone. There is constant interaction with the audience— taking questions, responding to comments. On my Facebook Live with Christine Devine, there were hundreds of questions and comments—so much so that we went over our planned time by more than thirty minutes! This conversation allowed me to answer questions in a much more comprehensive way and gain exposure to a new audience, many of whom started following me after seeing the interview.

In a time when books are going digital and tweets are all the rage, it's fascinating and encouraging to see new technology opening the door to longer, more in-depth discussion.

Podcasts

It's hard to imagine now but, before 2005, there were no podcasts. Not until Apple made them available on iTunes did anyone even imagine such a thing. Now podcasts are produced by everyone from major networks to teenagers with a dream. They range from quick updates on breaking news to deep explorations of issues, politics, science, and culture.

Without a doubt, they are exceptionally good forums for news, interviews, narratives, and entertainment. Not only do they provide an easy way for content creators to speak directly to their audience, but they give listeners a great way to expand their minds while they're on the move.

Whether you are just starting to develop your brand or a well-established rainmaker, these outlets can take you directly to the audience you hope to reach. Their easy access, combined with the enthusiasm of their listeners, is hard to beat. Podcasts can focus on very niche topics, as well as areas of broader interest. A quick search for the top podcasts in your niche is likely to show you relevant podcasts. In 2016, some of the top business podcasts were:

- **Dose of Leadership.** Richard Rierson, a former Marine whose first day as a commercial pilot was 9/11, interviews a range of experts and icons about excellence, truth, and common sense.
- **How I Built This.** Guy Raz interviews entrepreneurs about how they built their businesses from scratch and what obstacles they overcame on this NPR podcast.
- **Entrepreneur on Fire.** John Lee Dumas interviews successful entrepreneurs with a focus on the failures they faced and the lessons they learned, "Ah Ha!" moments in business, and how they turned that insight into success, ending with his six-question, rapid-fire Lightning Round.
- **The Tim Ferriss Show.** Tim Ferriss interviews world-renowned influencers, authors, celebrities, billionaires, and anyone else with valuable insights, skillfully eliciting the mental frameworks and life hacks they use to achieve so much more.
- **Smart Passive Income.** Pat Flynn is a renowned interviewer who is so transparent about his own business results that he shares his monthly income statement on his blog.
- **HBR IdeaCast.** Sarah Green, an editor at the *Harvard Business Review*, interviews impressive guests such as Stanford's Ronald Howard, a founder of decision analysis, and Google's Eric Schmidt, on this ideacast.[13]
- **The James Altucher Show.** James Altucher, a best-selling author, interviews a wide range of influencers in down-to-earth conversations about improving business, overcoming mental and emotional struggles, and making life better all around.[14]

Radio

With so many radio stations all around the country and the world, the best solution is for you to simply search for a list of radio shows in your area to find the best fit.

Don't discount the value or reach of Internet radio shows. Many have huge followings and have a range of guests that discuss broad issues. During National Autism Awareness Month in April, I frequently do interviews on health- and parenting-focused Internet radio shows, because they allow me to speak directly to parents, advocates, and others who work in the disability and autism community. VoiceAmerica.com has more than three hundred Internet radio shows that deliver hundreds of original programs weekly through eight channels focused on a range of topics from entertainment to sports. Appearances on one of their shows can provide you with branded contents that you can promote across your multiple social channels.

Almost every day, new Internet radio shows are popping up. A search for Internet radio shows about parenting alone brought up 355,000 results for me. If you have a moment now, why not check to see how many Internet radio shows there are in your niche? When you narrow the search to your region or with specific keywords, you can begin to build a list of go-to venues on Internet radio. Many of them will be local shows that are easier to get on than the top-rated national shows. When you're ready— and only if it suits your brand—you can start pitching shows like *The Steve Harvey Morning Show*, *The Tom Joyner Morning Show*, *The Rickey Smiley Morning Show*, or *The D. L. Hughley Show*.

Cable Networks

Viewership for the major cable networks is extremely high. Since not everyone realizes that big networks like CNN and

MSNBC are actually on cable—not broadcast networks—and Fox has both a television broadcast network and a cable network, I'm including a small selection of some of the networks on cable.

Do a little research in the category that suits your brand. Study the networks, the shows, the hosts, the issues, and the styles of your top prospects. Those who excel at this become experts in evaluating the best shows for their needs.

NEWS
Bloomberg
CNBC
CNN
Fox Business
Fox News
HLN
MSNBC

REGIONAL
News 12 Networks
NewsWatch 15

SPORTS
ESPN News
Fox Sports
MLB
NBA

ENTERTAINMENT
BBC America
MTV
USA

LIFESTYLE
Food Network
HGTV
Travel

Major Networks and Affiliates

Among the major networks, here are some of the shows that interview experts. Once you have a reel from cable shows, you can approach the major networks.

ABC
Good Morning America
The View
Nightline
ABC World News
20/20

CBS
Dr. Phil
The Early Show
The Doctors
CBS Morning New
CBS Evening News
Face the Nation

NBC
Today
Early Today
NBC Nightly News
Ellen
Dateline NBC
Meet the Press

FOX
The Wendy Williams Show
The Real
Fox News Sunday
Page Six TV
TMZ on TV

All the national broadcast networks have scores of local affiliates. If you Google "lists of ABC, NBC, or CBS television affiliates," you will be amazed by how many there are. In some cases, there are a dozen or more affiliate stations in any given state. Any of these may be viable options for you. NBC, for instance, has twenty-one affiliate stations in Texas alone.[15] CBS has almost the same number of affiliates in New York City as Montana.[16]

If your ideal audience is local, it makes sense to stay with the stations nearest you and your business. If it's national, you can pitch any of these networks as well as cable stations. All of them have audiences across the country. This allows you to expand your potential exponentially and reach a new audience.

You may never have watched WJAR-TV, the NBC affiliate in Rhode Island, but it's been around since 1949 and has the fourth-highest viewership in New England. WJAR also happens to be the only local channel that offers 7:00 p.m. news.[17]

While this book is not about the career path for news anchors or commentators contracted by TV stations, it is clear that many TV professionals have seen local affiliates like WJAR as stepping-stones to higher-profile appearances on the major networks. Meteorologist Dylan Dreyer, CNN Chief International Correspondent Christiane Amanpour, and ESPN anchor Steve Berthiaume all made early appearances at WJAR.[18] TV experts can just as easily make use of local affiliates to gain experience, create a local following, and build an impressive interview reel that gives them more options at other networks.

Amazing as it seems now with so many channels to watch at

any hour of the day or night, for thirty years (1956–1986), only three major commercial television networks existed: ABC, CBS, and NBC. Today the "Big Three" networks combined control only about 32 percent of the market.[19] Since Fox has had similar ratings since the late 1990s, some believe it deserves to be a part of a new category: the "Big Four."

Every year the competition from other "on-air" networks grows. The available slots of TV experts grows right along with it. These are only a sampling of the shows airing in each of these broadcast categories.

COMMERCIAL
NBC
CBS
ABC
Fox
The CW

NEWS & LIFESTYLE
Ion Life
Justice Network
Live Well
TBD

PUBLIC TELEVISION
PBS World
France 24
MiND
NHK World

SPANISH NETWORKS
Telemundo
Univision
UniMás

Azteca
Estrella TV

GENRE
MyNetworkTV
MeTV
Soul of the South
Family Channel

With so many choices, few of us realize how big the scope of possibilities is. And the opportunities are growing every day. Whether you start out on local stations and make your way up to the national networks, or whether you are lucky enough to find your ideal audience in the more accessible local markets, so many options are out there just waiting for you on major television networks, cable networks, radio, podcasts, and live streams. Every single one of them can—and must be—leveraged on social media to amplify your impact thousands of times over.

CHAPTER 7

Jump on Breaking News Stories

The absolute best way to launch your career as an expert is by inserting yourself into a breaking news story.

A fire breaks out in Calabasas near Los Angeles. Hundreds of brave firefighters rush to battle the blaze as it races through the hills in ninety-degree heat. Mandatory evacuation of thousands of residents in Topanga Canyon and the Mulholland Highway region is underway.

Producers on national and local TV stations go to high alert. Hitting Google, Facebook, Twitter, YouTube, and anything else they can think of, producers rush to find experts who can explain what's happening or even bring an inside perspective to set their story apart. People who have lost their homes or officials from the LA County Fire Department would be the obvious choices, but they've got bigger things on their minds right now.

Scanning local news online and TV, producers look for keywords to enhance their search. They scan their list of contacts, calling anyone who seems relevant, and check their inboxes for pitches from experts and publicists offering to appear on the show.

At the same time, it's vitally important to keep tabs on any fresh angles their competitors bring to the story. When the grounds of Camp Wildcraft burn and fifty children lose out on

summer camp, one local outlet hits pay dirt, interviewing a con-
cerned eyewitness with a stake in the outcome of the story.

"I am kind of in despair at the moment," says Shari Davis,
who owns the camp with her husband. "It looks like the whole
area could be destroyed."[1]

As charred power poles knock out power to 681 homes, Robert Villegas appears as an expert, speaking for the local power
company, Southern California Edison, to let people know that the
power is being restored. Then Joe Sirard, an expert meteorologist
from the National Weather Service, explains that temperatures
were ten to twenty degrees higher than average when the fire
started, but are expected to be cooler the next day.[2]

When the story breaks, some of these experts are contacted
within seconds. If you can get a pitch with three solid talking
points in a producer's hands, it could be the break you need to go
on TV as an expert and get your message out.

Most of the experts you see on TV have done exactly that. No
matter how famous they are or how many times they've been on a
particular show, there is no guarantee that a harried producer will
think of them first when she's racing to fill slots on the show.

As a media-savvy expert, you need to develop a pitch the
moment you see a breaking news story that matches your expertise. You want to let her know you've got what she's looking for.
By sending her a strong pitch, you're saying:

> "I'm an expert. I'm already engaged with this story.
> "Here's how I can add value. And I'm ready right
> now!"

I can't repeat it enough: Whatever you can do to make life easier for the producers will always work in your favor. Sending a
solid pitch to a producer at a moment of crisis is a great way to do
that.

But you've got to be quick. The story is taking place in real time. Most likely, there are only a handful of minutes to fill. If you want to get in the game, make your move.

Keep in mind, most stories have a twenty-four- to forty-eight-hour life span. Assume you've got twelve hours—up to twenty-four hours at the most—to get on. After that, unless it's the kind of outsized story that takes over the media all week, it's old news.

The news cycles are so fast now, you've got to really be current on everything that's being said. It's as if you're jumping onto a moving train. You want to insert yourself into an existing story and make yourself a part of it.

Your Take on Breaking News

All stories happen in the context of something bigger. When news breaks about a high-profile custody case, there are obvious legal issues to discuss, but a host or guest may also raise questions about the celebrities involved, the cost to children caught up in protracted custody battles, or the way the fame of one parent can affect the decisions of a judge. It's not enough for me to know the nuances of the legal arguments, the Constitution, immigration laws, and precedents set by the courts. I also need to be prepared to give my opinion about how a case might play out in any number of other ways—how it impacts people, how it plays out politically, or how it changes our perspective on the private lives of celebrities.

A rainmaker doesn't just recite facts. It's your job to find an interesting angle, a unique point of view, a distinctive voice to bring to the discussion.

If you ever watch CNN on Saturday mornings, you may have seen me on the *Smerconish* show. This fast-paced news show is hosted by lawyer and radio talk show host Michael Smerconish. He brings an East Coast edge to his interviews, and he likes to bring on guests with strong personalities to match wits.

After Vanderbilt law professor Carol Swain and I locked horns, Mike realized he had hit pay dirt! Carol and I are both experienced attorneys with incredibly strong opinions who happen to be diametrically opposed. When the two of us are on, the producers of the show can expect not only a substantive legal discussion but also a spirited debate.

Once they saw how our clashing opinions invigorated the show, the producers took every opportunity to bring us on together. When a California college student ran an ad seeking only roommates who were African-American, it went viral. Carol and I both felt strongly about it, but we disagreed. When college protests against police brutality were breaking news, the Smerconish producers reached out to Carol and me again. In preinterviews with both of us on both stories, the producers confirmed that we had very different opinions and were passionate about the issues of these stories.

When I learned that Carol would be the guest I would appear with, I read everything I could about her, including the books she had written and the courses she had taught while a professor at Vanderbilt Law School. I checked her social media sites and even spoke with law school colleagues who knew her. I wanted to be prepared and, if possible, anticipate the points she might make— particularly since she teaches law for a living. I needed to be at the top of my game. I needed to be sure of the facts while figuring out how to best position my opinions, since I knew Carol would challenge just about everything I said. I didn't want any surprise.

When we were on the air, I suggested that the student who posted the ad had some legitimate concerns. My take was that the ad was a cry for help from a vulnerable young student, not intentionally discriminatory. As expected, Carol jumped all over me. She said I had a double standard and frankly doubted I would have the same opinion if the student wasn't African-American. I fired back that she had missed the point. The student had expressed feelings of isolation. Even the college president had acknowledged that this was a real issue for many minority students.

Our verbal sparring went on for almost five minutes with

occasional comments and questions from Smerconish. In the end, we both made salient points, stood our ground, and delivered a segment that the audience and producers loved. Needless to say, we've both been invited back many more times.

Never be afraid to assert your point of view and allow it to shine during media interviews. You can expect other guests to do the same.

Rainmakers know that having an opinion is how they distinguish themselves. Not all the *Smerconish* show viewers agree with me or with Carol. My own supportive friends and fans sometimes ask me why the network has her on so often, given what they believe to be her outlandishly conservative positions. The response is simple: She has strong opinions! Audiences know that when they see us on CNN or any other network, they can count on both of us to be informed and impassioned.

More than ever, shows are booking experts with conflicting opinions as Smerconish often does with Carol Swain and me. Audiences want to hear both sides, and conflict makes for great TV. In these types of interviews, the hosts or a reporter will provide the background facts. There will often be a video package or other interviews at the scene that are played before the live interview begins. Remember, in this scenario, you are not there to repeat what has already been presented by the host or the video package. A rainmaker brings more than just good information or statistics in their field to a story. They don't just recite facts. They bring passion. There's an angle in the story that aligns with their theme.

With advances in data crunching, the media outlets themselves are focusing more tightly on specific themes as well. It's a trend that shapes the media at every level.

Jessica Coen, executive editor of Mashable, says it's even affecting what breaking news stories they cover. In 2005, Peter Cashmore's Mashable blog was "the one-stop shop" for social media. Now it is targeted exclusively to culture, tech, and entertainment. They used to assume their audience was all tech lovers or anyone in a certain age bracket. Then research showed that their best targets were "superfans," early adopters who liked to binge-watch shows on Netflix. The results were incredibly specific. Their most avid fans were people who were "interested in *Game of Thrones*, but not the recap of the episode, ... interested in fan theories and smarter angles about what's going to happen next, ... [who loved] to hear about Elon Musk and whether or not we'll get to Mars."[3]

When Mashable stopped generalizing and made their stories more specific, the difference was dramatic. The average story on Mashable is now shared 4,977 times—more than twice as often as before.[4]

Making their brand, angle, and point of view more specific had another advantage. It set them apart. Instead of constantly trying to get ahead of formidable competitors like the Verge, Recode, and Gizmodo, their clearly defined brand took them out of the competition.[5] They became the go-to source for a very specific niche, and it's really paid off.

Whatever media expertise you build, think long and hard about how to make your brand and point of view specific enough that it will set you apart from all the other doctors, lawyers, chefs, teachers, athletes, and other experts out there competing for the same slot.

Bring Your Brand

Matching your niche to breaking news stories is just the beginning. Once you've got the story, marry it to your point of view so you can express an opinion that links to your brand. Once you hone in on your brand, you will able to use to it expand your expertise to a surprising range of topics.

As you read in Chapter 2, Dr. Drew shifted his brand from focusing on his training as an internal medicine doctor to human behavior. He started out doing shows about rehab and substance abuse. Those issues were a good fit for his medical credentials, but he noticed very quickly that what hooked him in the story of a drug-crazed girl killing her boyfriend was human behavior. The moment he heard the story, he asked himself, "What would drive someone to commit such a heinous act?"

By making his brand human behavior and not just focusing on the medical angle, he could segue into breaking news stories and even legal stories. It gives him legitimacy in commenting on stories like that, even though he's not a lawyer or psychologist. His brand lets him cut across a wider range of topics than listing "MD" on his résumé would ever do. It allows him to avoid being pigeonholed and makes him more marketable as an expert, too.

I've talked a lot about my brand throughout the book. When I am pitching a breaking news story, I am always looking for an angle to jump into the story, I ask myself: Does the story have a legal issue? Given my law degree and legal experience, that can automatically give me an angle that separates me from other experts who may have something to contribute.

Next I ask: Can I bring my knowledge and experiences as a parent? As a special needs parent? As a nonprofit and for-profit business owner who has made her way out of a poor community and understands overcoming obstacles and defying odds? Whether it's a high-profile celebrity custody battle over adopted children or indictments of government officials in Flint, Michigan, over poisonous water, I am looking for ways to educate and empower the audience. By always staying on brand, producers know that I am a reliable voice when they need strong points of view on women's rights, children's issues, and social justice stories.

When I talk to the audiences after a show, people often come up to me and say, "You're so empowering! I feel inspired." That's exactly what I'm going for. If you watch a show I'm on, you're going to be clear about my opinion. Whether I'm talking about a medical issue on *The Doctors* or children in need, I lead with a strong opinion and work to empower people. I bring in advocacy whenever I can because that's a part of my brand. So even if I do an entire show without ever saying "empower," "inspire," or "advocate," people feel it.

You don't always have to be explicit in stating your message. You certainly don't have to be the rudest or the loudest. But if you come on the air with no opinion at all, you'll be forgotten. No one will remember you. The odds are good you won't be invited back. But what's worse, you'll have missed a golden opportunity to share your message.

Tricks of the Trade

Today the 24/7 demand for content never lets up. Keeping your finger on the digital pulse of your niche is vital. Watch the shows that are a good match for your brand. Know what aired this week, last week, and the week before. Get a feel for what the shows' hosts and producers like. Follow them on social media to see what kind of things they post and respond to with enthusiasm.

Breaking news stories always interrupt regularly scheduled programming, but producers try to fill the other slots well ahead of time by putting out the word in the industry. If you subscribe to services like Cision and PRWeb, you can get inside information about what kind of content producers expect to air on any given week along with contact information for those producers. The producers looking for content and guests will not be the executive producer, who functions as the CEO of the show. Instead, you will more likely see them simply listed as producers, and possibly segment producers, associate producers, or assistant producers.

Never contact the host of a show about getting an interview on a segment. Think about it. That would mean asking an extremely busy, higher-ranking person to do your job for you. You'd also be asking them to expend their own professional capital with that producer, when you know nothing about the political climate on the show. Beyond that, you have no real idea how much clout that host has with any given producer. Why wade into all that?

Pitch the producer. It's their job to book guests on the show. If the show has a clearly defined segment that is always the same, such as "lifestyle" or "news," it makes sense to pitch the producers of that segment.

Keep in mind that producers change. There is a constant shuffle in the media, with people taking over new positions, moving to different shows, or performing a completely different function. This mobility can really work to your advantage. If you make a point to network well, the producers, directors, hosts, and crew of a single show may soon be calling you from other shows, as they move around the industry. I've had it happen many times myself.

Make a point to follow everyone who covers your niche with authority: TV hosts, producers, analysts, journalists, bloggers, even other media experts. Follow as many of them as you can. You'll always learn something new, whether it's tips on a breaking news story, new angles on the story, better ways to write your posts, how often to post, or people they follow that you should be following, too.

Don't stop there. Your goal is always to create engagement—not only with your followers and viewers, but also with producers, hosts, and journalists. When they post a link to a story in your niche, post a comment that adds real value, offering insights or pointing out other aspects of the story. Include a link to your own blog or website, if you've said more about it there.

Start with the people you recognize, but build out this invaluable knowledge base as quickly as you can. It's one of your best resources. Google the relevant keywords for your niche. Follow your competitors. Read the top bloggers. Watch what people are saying in chat rooms and forums. Bring in as many diverse voices as you can. Set out to be the best-informed person in the room about what's going on in your niche.

Rainmakers continually search for new sources, new connections, and new insights into their market. They always need to know the current thinking, both pros and cons. How can you join the conversation and influence its flow if you don't know what's already being said?

If you get on TV with a host or expert who holds an opposing point of view, you need to not only be aware of that perspective, but be ready to defend your position in a clear, engaging voice.

The clock on that story starts ticking from the moment it hits the news. It's only going to be relevant as long as it's in the news cycle. So you've got to know what those cycles are and stay on top of them. That means getting media alerts for the topics that you're ready to talk about.

You can't just follow major mainstream news. In a competitive market, you need *an edge*!

If you hope to establish yourself as an expert on celebrity news, you can find celebrity stories in *People*, *USA Today*, the *Los Angeles Times*, and other mainstream publications. But that's not where you're going to get daily updates on the latest things that are happening.

If you're a sports commentator, your specialty is even more niche. It's not just sports, but a specific sport. Charles Barkley calls basketball games—not football, not hockey, not soccer—he's a basketball expert. He played basketball, then parlayed that knowledge into being a pundit who gives well-informed opinions about professional basketball. He lives, eats, and breathes basketball. You can be sure he doesn't just tune into ESPN and the six o'clock news to find out what's happening in basketball. He's watching online streaming, and getting up-to-the-minute alerts for all the news in basketball twenty-four hours a day.

Media Is Rapidly Changing

There's no time to waste. Tectonic shifts are taking place in the American news.

Old forms of media are fading. Legacy news outlets, such as the *New York Times*, are expanding to virtual reality journalism to let consumers experience the news live. MIT and others are developing new, more personal ways to tell stories in digital formats. Soon all the major networks will be following suit. It's a time of dynamic change.

The 24/7 news cycle has taken over so quickly that few people have had time to register how revolutionary—and how accessible—this exciting opportunity is.

- 12 new users join social media every second—*1 million new users every day.*[6]
- 43 percent of mobile users say they are viewing more news than ever before.[7]
- 55 percent of U.S. smartphone users get daily news alerts.[8]
- 57 percent of TV viewers care most about local news.[9]
- 62 percent of users over thirty (and nearly *all* users under thirty) go to social media for news.[10]
- 142 seconds is the length of the average evening news story package.[11]

In the last ten years there has been such a proliferation of news outlets that literally hundreds of thousands of hours need to be filled with content.

The pressure intensifies with breaking news stories. Whether it's a natural disaster, a plane crash, or a mass shooting, news rooms have to respond in real time to their audiences' demand for information and explanations.

When these stories break, previously scheduled programs are pushed aside and stations go into high gear to deliver up-to-the-minute reports. Inevitably, they have a small amount of footage from a disaster, an attack, or another emergency, and then they have to wait for more details from the scene. We're all familiar with what happens while they wait. They fill the time with discussions and interviews with experts about the incident.

In a perfect world, people involved in the story would be available to discuss it, but this is rarely possible. The next best thing is an expert with the background and experience to explain to viewers exactly what's happening and what the implications are.

As soon as a story breaks, producers immediately start looking for someone credible, engaging, and available on short notice. The experts we see on the air were available and prepared to confidently jump into the conversation to add value in a way that helps move the story forward.

After El Niño results in major flooding in Los Angeles, a flood risk assessment expert may come on the air to talk about the risks and best responses. When shots are fired on a vehicle in Chicago, a paramedic or a former police officer may come on to provide viewers with insight into what happens in this kind of shooting. In a crisis, producers are often unable to talk to the people directly involved, so they invite related experts who can provide more general information. In some instances, experts bring a sense of calm to chaotic situations.

Experts like these play an important role in helping producers advance their stories. Appearing on these shows can also make an expert's reputation. With stiff competition among network, cable, and digital outlets, a new expert is born every day.

Get in the Game!

By the time a breaking news story appears on the major networks, the top media experts are already on it. Here's what they do:

- **Split-Second News**: Monitor keywords, search hashtags, get Google alerts, watch trends, track bloggers and journalists, follow media outlets. (More ahead on how you can do this.)
- **Brand Agility**: Quickly recognize the ways a story matches—or doesn't match—their brand. They ruthlessly

ignore the ones that don't. Excellence means learning not to waste your time trying to make things fit. Identify the network, shows, and relevant producers that match your expertise. You can often contact the assignment desk at a news station to find the booker or producer. Also read the credits at the end of a targeted show—the producers' names are listed. If their e-mails are not identified on the show's website, use your knowledge of how e-mail addresses are normally assigned to ferret out the correct e-mail.

- **Pitch Hard and Fast:** Craft an irresistible hook, an angle, and three talking points in record time, then shoot an e-mail to several producers simultaneously. Practicing this like a card trick any time you watch the news is the best way to get fast.
- **Engage the Story:** Immediately get your take out there. Tweet with a hashtag that's already trending. Post a blog with your point of view. Send a real-time media alert. Go on Facebook Live to share your angle and insights. Think of it as pitching producers, who are already scouring social media for connections. It's not uncommon for producers to see my posts and call me when a story breaks.
- **Rinse and Repeat:** Make a habit of getting in the game until it's like second nature to you. Influence is built on trustworthy, consistent participation. You won't get invited on every show you pitch. Nobody does. But you can always get your voice out there, share your point of view, and do it all again tomorrow.

Media Alerts

Media alerts can give you an edge. They let you know the instant a story breaks.

It would be meaningless for me to recommend one app over another here, because as we speak, new methods for receiving those alerts are being developed. In a single month, January 2016, more than fifty thousand new apps were submitted to iTunes.[12] By the time you read this book, thousands more will have hit the market. Stay on top of reviews for the leading apps to be sure you're getting the best, fastest, most comprehensive information available in the way that suits you best. The world we live in gets more interesting by the day.

As of this writing, Google Alerts is still one of the most popular ways to track keywords and phrases related to your brand. When anything comes out in the news, blogs, videos, chat rooms, books, or other online venues, an alert will be sent to you by e-mail. If it's breaking news, you'll want to go online immediately to see what's been said and where so you can plan your next move.

One of the reasons it's become so popular is that it's remarkably easy to use. If you find that you are receiving too many alerts in the course of a day, you can quickly reduce the volume in the settings. If your search parameters are too wide, you can experiment with other keywords that narrow the focus. It's an invaluable tool for media experts who need to stay in the know. Here's how to use it:

Google Alerts

- **Web Address:** Go to http://www.google.com/alerts/.
- **Search Query:** Fill in the keywords or phrases you want to track.
- **Result Type:** Choose the places you want to search (news, blogs, video, chat rooms, books, etc.).
- **How Often:** "As it happens," "once a day," and "once a week" are options.
- **How Many:** Choose "only the best results" or "everything."
- **Deliver To:** Fill in your e-mail address.
- **Create Alert:** Click the big red button.

Google Trends is another way to keep your finger on the digital pulse. You can find out what's being searched for and talked about most in the past hour, the past day, or the past several years. Checking Google Trends allows you to do background research, looking into how long a topic has been trending and when it spiked. Like Google Alerts, you'll find it very easy to use:

Google Trends

- **Web Address:** Go to https://trends.google.com/trends/.
- **Explore Topics:** Enter keywords or phrases.
- **Worldwide:** Go international or narrow the search by country.
- **Past 5 Years:** Customize the time span from years ago to "past hour."
- **All Categories:** Accept all categories, or narrow your search.
- **Web Search:** Select "web," "image," "news," "shopping," or "YouTube."

If you want to establish yourself as the go-to expert in your niche, you need to educate yourself on what's going on in your field up-to-the-minute. If I'm on *Dr. Phil* to speak about a missing child, someone in the audience might mention a similar case that was all over the news a few years back. If I have never heard about that case, it's much harder to speak with authority about whether it's relevant to our discussion or not.

So you need to read about what's going on in your industry and especially your niche, even if it doesn't have anything to do with your business directly. Because I am putting myself forward as a legal expert, I make a practice of constantly reading legal journals and papers. Obviously, I stay on top of the legal stories that make headlines in the newspapers or start trending online.

Make Yourself the Go-To Expert

Every time you appear as an expert on TV, radio, podcasts, and other venues, you establish yourself more firmly as a recognized expert in your field. When you repost those appearances, as you'll learn to do in the social media chapters in Part IV, you'll amplify that perception further.

There's more you can do to make yourself the first name—the go-to expert—that comes to mind when a topic in your niche comes up. When you achieve "go-to expert" status, producers will start calling you first. But you've got to lay the groundwork.

It's no accident that Rachel Maddow has become a go-to political commentator with the second highest number of total viewers in prime time for years on end.[13]

Maddow got her first break by winning a contest to find a new sidekick for the host of *The Dave in the Morning Show* on WRNX radio in Amherst, Massachusetts. "They didn't hire me because I had a strong interest in the news," she says. "They hired me because I had a nice voice and I was willing to get up that early."[14] But she kept working to establish herself as a well-informed, fair-minded commentator with a strong point of view.

Six years later, in 2005, she had her own radio show; two years after that, *The Rachel Maddow Show* debuted on MSNBC.[15] All along the way she took every opportunity to establish herself as a political expert. MSNBC President Phil Griffin says, "Rachel is informed, she does her homework, she preps better and longer than anyone, she is fair and always smart."[16]

In 2011 she famously hurt Michael Moore's feelings when she postponed his interview on her show. Jimmy Carter, former CIA interrogator Ali Soufan, and Michael Moore had all been scheduled to appear, but Maddow told her producers, "I can't read three books this weekend. I can only read two." When Moore learned the reason, he exclaimed, "*Nobody* reads the book!" But Maddow does.[17]

If you want to be the best, be the best. Educate yourself. Stay current on the issues. Know more about your topic than the other people calling themselves experts. Be the one who reads the book.

Once you've done that, you can craft informed opinions and get them out there. You may not have or want your own TV show. You may not even have given your first interview. But that's no reason to keep your insights to yourself. There are countless ways to get your message out: posting comments on videos and your own Facebook Live stream, writing articles, adding your take to your own blog and website, or posting and commenting on ongoing discussions on social media, to name a few.

When a fast-moving news story breaks, producers and journalists immediately check expert blogs and social media posts, while Google Alerts start pinging their inboxes. They search for the hashtags that ignite like a brushfire with trending news. If the story's in your niche, they're looking for you!

If you haven't been building an online presence by commenting on related news stories, making your opinion known in articles and blogs, they won't be able to find you.

You can reach them with a pitch. With strong talking points and relevant credentials, you can still capture their attention, but you will make it much easier for the producers to invite you on if you show up as an expert when they go online to check you out.

Hiring a Publicist

Once you have enough experience to appear polished and professional and you are ready to expand your presence, it may be time to hire a publicist to approach producers for you. The most effective publicists will not consider taking you on unless you're committed to appearing regularly and you have a great press kit with a solid collection of clips in your reel. As I mentioned in Chapter 4, a publicist usually charges a monthly retainer. Their fee may be as little as $1,500 or as high as $10,000 a month, depending on the market.

Good publicists have spent years developing the kind of relationships you want to start developing, too. They can pitch you to their contacts, but you still have to find the stories and come up with the talking points yourself. So even though they may make the actual contacts with bookers and producers, you still need to do everything you're learning in this book. The publicist may change the pitch to third person ("She's a surgeon" instead of "I'm a surgeon"), but they are not the experts.

You are the expert. The publicist doesn't know the facts or talking points. They will also need your research to help choose the shows that match your brand. Your publicist will just be leveraging those materials with their connections. You have to research the stories and provide the substance to the publicist every time: "Here's what I can add to this breaking news story. This is my opinion about this child abduction case or this sudden drop in the Dow." You're still driving the pitches.

In 2014 there was a peak in coverage about police brutality—an issue I was passionate about that was directly linked to my brand. It was important to me to inform people and get my message out.

I hired a publicist and told her I wanted to do a big push to insert myself into this major breaking news coverage. We ramped everything up, doing more pitches for a wider range of shows. I took on a full commitment to make myself available to appear. Sometimes I was going on the air morning, noon, and night.

The news was covering police shootings and protests around the clock. The issue had sparked a revolt in people, and there was a voracious appetite for these stories and commentary by experts weighing in. If you were a civil rights lawyers, there was a real need for your expertise.

I would get up every morning at 5:00 a.m. and read my seven newspapers online to see which A, B, and C stories were hot. "What's going on in the news cycle of the day? What are they focusing on? Does that big Supreme Court decision have a bearing on this?" When I noticed something they weren't mentioning, I'd do background research and come up with talking points.

By 8:00 a.m., I'd call the publicist and we'd brainstorm together, running through pitches together, then deciding who to pitch before she got off the phone to start making calls. We got into a rhythm.

Because of that big push, I got on more shows that year than I ever had before. We took my media appearances to a completely new level, which made a huge impact on my business and brand. The exposure from those appearances drove new clients to my door. I saw a major increase in calls from prospects, many of whom became new clients for my firm. The increased exposure raised my recognition value. Producers started to call. I found that the hosts already expected the good comments from me when I appeared as an expert. It was more than name recognition value for my brand; that burst took me to the next level.

When you're ready, it's worth the time, effort, and expense to make a big push.

PART IV

AMPLIFY IT!

CHAPTER 8

Forget the Old Social Media

I f you ask me, social media is the greatest invention of all time. It allows you to have a presence online for very little money. You can amplify your message without spending a dime. And you'll have a lot of fun while you're at it!

Social media never sleeps. With more than 3.2 billion people online around the world, this is what happens on social media *every minute of the day*:

- Facebook users Like more than 4.1 million posts.
- Instagram users Like more than 1.7 million photos.
- Twitter users tweet more than 347,000 times.
- YouTube users upload 300 hours of video.[1]

Letting people know about your brand is so much easier now than what we did in—OK, I'll call it "the old days"—when you had to slap a big ad on a billboard or the side of a bus. Now, with social media, we can have live conversations with thousands of people at any time, day or night. We can humanize our products, weave in great stories, and actually *engage* our customers while we get our message out to more people than ever before.

Your Audience Is Waiting

Not long ago who could've imagined the power of a 140-character tweet?

Twitter didn't exist before the summer of 2006. Facebook expanded beyond its Ivy League base a few months later. By 2008 Facebook had 100 million users.[2] Twitter hit that mark in 2012.[3]

In April 2005, YouTube had already started letting people post videos for free. Today it generates $4 billion annually.[4] The number of YouTube channels earning six figures goes up 50 percent a year.[5]

In 2010, twenty-seven-year-old Kevin Systrom built an iPhone app to check in with friends, meet up, and post pictures—a kind of "instant telegram" he ultimately called Instagram. When it went live in October 2010, he and his partner, twenty-five-year-old Brazilian engineer Mike Krieger, figured they'd have at least six hours before anything happened, so they could get some sleep. But the downloads started pouring in from all around the world in minutes.[6]

"We crossed 10,000 users within hours, and I was like, 'This is the best day of my life!'" Systrom said. "At the end of the day, it kept growing so much I thought, 'Are we counting wrong?'"[7]

By the end of the week one hundred thousand people had downloaded Instagram. The same thing happened the next week. In two months, they had 1 million users.[8]

"It was both rewarding and humbling to see people embrace Instagram as both a new home on their iPhone—and a new way of communicating visually with people around the world," Systrom said.[9] The very concept of imagining a "home" on your phone would've been alien to all of us a decade ago. Now social media is where people live and breathe.

Just 551 days after Instagram was launched, in April 2012, Facebook bought the start-up for $1 billion—though it had never made a cent.[10]

Instagram is rapidly becoming one of the most popular social networks worldwide. Already it has 600 million active users[11]—almost twice as many as Twitter.

It is the preferred social network of teens and young adults, with 50 percent of its users under thirty years old. If you wonder whether or not this is a market worth pursuing, keep in mind that 67 percent of the luxury retail brands on social media have Instagram profiles. They have discovered that it's a lucrative market.

Snapchat also attracts a young demographic. The average user is sixteen years old.[12] When Facebook offered to buy it for $3 billion, Snapchat turned it down. In March 2017, its IPO valuation was $24 billion.[13] As Bloomberg reported, "Even if you're over thirty, you can't ignore Snapchat anymore."[14]

At the same time, LinkedIn, which used to feature interactive groups for professionals to crowdsource new ideas, share points of view, and build networks, has started to look like a ghost town.[15]

TOP SOCIAL NETWORKS
Number of Active Users in the Millions (January 2017)

Facebook									1,871
YouTube							1,325		
Instagram			600						
Twitter		317							
SnapChat		300							
LinkedIn	106								

Source: "Leading Social Networks Worldwide as of January 2017, Ranked by Number of Active Users." Statistica. https://www.statista.com/statistics/272014/global-social-networks-ranked-by-number-of-users/. Also: "YouTube Company Statistics." Statistic Brain Research Institute. Sept 1, 2016. http://www.statisticbrain.com/youtube-statistics/

A Social Way of Life

Get engaged! Social media is not just a means to an end, it's a way of life.

Think carefully about your brand, your intentions, and your goals before you launch a presence on social media. Whether you establish a business brand or a personal brand, there is no question that it has the potential to dramatically increase your market value, but it also gives you a greater responsibility.

As Glenn Llopis of *Forbes* says, it is "a never-ending journey that extends well beyond social media.... [It] is about making a full-time commitment to the journey of defining yourself as a leader" and how that shapes the way you bring value to others.[16]

Think of your social media presence as a way to represent the value you consistently deliver to your followers. While you may share your achievements, your upcoming appearances, your awards, your offers, and your success stories, the level of influence you develop relies on using those posts to craft a voice that others can depend on.

Every day I start my morning looking at my seven favorite newspapers on my phone. When a story's hot, I start tweeting about it. If you see me on social, you know that 5:00 a.m. tweets are not unusual. I know that this is the time that many show producers and bookers are checking social feeds and making decisions about their lineups for the day. So I want to make sure that if there is a story aligned with my brand, I am weighing in on the story as those decisions are being made. I recently started appearing on a show in the UK because producers in London saw my tweets about a story where they needed an expert comment.

As a legal and social issues expert, I know people are expecting to hear my opinion. Those who follow me want to know what I think. Many will send me a tweet or leave a post on my Facebook page. Those comments are very valuable to me, as they give me a sense of how people are responding to a particular story, and I always enjoy engaging with my followers.

Social media is a two-way conversation. It's not old-school advertising—a big billboard shouting:

"HIRE ME!"
"BUY WHAT I'M SELLING!"

You're saying, "I have some information I think you'll find valuable, and I want to share it with you. What can I do to better inform you? How can I help you become more educated about this topic?" Social media is the only place you can have these kinds of real-time, open, interactive discussions with not only producers and bookers, but also with people who have shared interests.

Can you see now why I love social media? It makes things happen!

Before You Post

The most surefire way to fail is to post things on social media without a strategy. You'll waste your time because you lack direction. Since you don't know what to focus on, you'll almost certainly miss the best opportunities that come your way. Most of the benefits that come from knowing your audience will dissipate because your random posts will bring in people who are unrelated to your brand. In the end, it will be much easier for competitors with solid social media strategies to build the platform you could've built from those followers.[17]

The first thing you need to do is make sure you're easy to find by getting your name right. If you've started out on social media with a nickname, you've either got to dump the nickname or make it your brand. Names like these may have sounded good at the time, but you've got to ask yourself if they advance your brand or not.

Ah Choo
Imina Rush
Ancestors 8
Wok Din
Gotdeswag
BreakerBreakerl

If your social media name is not your name or the name of your business, it's the wrong name. How will people find you?

If you get an interview on TV, and the producer appreciates your input on a breaking news story enough to tag you when they post, they're going to use your name. If it doesn't link to your site, they will not go looking for you. The moment has passed and you've missed out. Make yourself easy to find.

Once you've got the right name in place, you need to think strategically about what you'll post. Ask yourself these questions:

What Is the Story of Your Brand?

Let your followers get to know you by telling them what brought you here and why your message means so much to you. Your story should be short but emotionally compelling. It's not so much about sharing the personal moment when you first decided to develop your business or describing your process as it is about getting to the heart of the matter. And it's not all about you. The story of your brand should also answer the questions you're asked most often when you tell people about your brand.

The GoPro story by CEO Nicholas Woodman is accompanied by a video on gopro.com/about-us.

> We have passionate ideas about what's possible in this world....
>
> GoPro helps people capture and share their lives' most meaningful experiences with others—to cele-

brate them together. Like how a day on the mountain with friends is more meaningful than one spent alone, the sharing of our collective experiences makes our lives more fun....

Enabling you to share your life through incredible photos and videos is what we do.

This is your life...GoPro.[18]

The story introducing Shonda Rhimes's "Make Great Television" class on MasterClass.com is brief, but effective:

When Shonda Rhimes pitched *Grey's Anatomy* she got so nervous she had to start over. Twice. Since then, she has created and produced TV's biggest hits. In her class, Shonda teaches you how to create compelling characters, write a pilot, pitch your idea, and stand out in the writers' room....Welcome to Shondaland.[19]

What Is Your Content Strategy?

Generally, leaders in the field of social media have proven that it is content that educates and engages your audience, serves their need, and builds your authority as the go-to expert who is successful. When it comes to what to post and when, why start from zero when other influencers or companies like yours have already honed in on strategies that work? Even companies like Coca-Cola, with the resources to do any kind of marketing in the world, focus the bulk of their strategy and resources on providing good content to consumers, because it yields the best marketing results. That is a sign that their vast marketing studies have shown that content strategies are the most effective. We can benefit from their research!

It's like an investor choosing to invest in the same companies as the legendary investor Warren Buffett. It's why dynamic small businesses and book authors eager to create breakthroughs in marketing often say, "When in doubt, copy Tim Ferriss!" The best influencers, the most effective business owners, and your most successful competition are the people to watch. You won't be able to get in the game at their level. But you can almost always emulate their content strategy—to save yourself the trial-and-error and expensive studies they had to do.

To develop your strategy, start by evaluating what the leaders in your field are doing. Sites like BuzzSumo (mentioned earlier), Bird-Song Analytics, Likealyzer, Klear, and many others can quickly give you an in-depth analysis of their content. It will show you exactly which posts and updates have generated the most engagement. Look at the way the posts are worded. What topics stir up interest best? How many times a day do they post? What is the ratio of original posts to shared content? What hashtags are used? How often does the influencer respond to comments and, when they do, what do they say?

From this information, you can put together a content strategy template that has already proven effective. That's your starting point. Then you need to fill-in your strategy with information about who your audience is, where they hang out, what's important to them, and what they like enough to share.

The old-school approach was to simply focus on quality content, wrongly assuming that most people would share the same opinions about what was high quality and what wasn't. In that model, a content strategy involved a lot of guesses about what to post, how often to post, and which posts were likely to be most effective.

The new model replaces guesses with testing.

What Topics, Events, and Information Matter Most to Your Target Audience?

One of the great benefits of social media is that you can not only get responses, but you can easily find out what's trending, where people are going, who they like, what they listen to, and what they post or repost. As Google and Facebook well know, this information is so valuable, empires can be built on it.

As the old sales adage goes: "It's simple. Find out what people want and give it to them."

What are the people in your target audience looking for? What do they need? What problems can you help them solve? Harvard Business School professor Clayton Christensen says that most companies try to improve sales by adding special features, improving functions, or lowering the prices on their products. But your follower "simply has a job to be done and is seeking the best product or service to do it."[20]

Share Brand-Related Events

If you're at a march, a big convention, a trade show, or any big event where a lot of people are posting, be sure to add the trending hashtag. Immediately, it connects you with everyone else who is engaged by the event. It's a great way to expand your following.

As simple as this may seem, my friend and social media consultant, Brian Ross Adams, and I are often amazed at how often we attend big events with high-profile brands, where there is little to no social media activity around the event. In some cases, we are the only people posting! Even people with überbrands constantly miss great opportunities to promote those brands. Corporations understand how important it is. That's why, when they sign up celebrities or influencers for endorsement deals, there is a contractual requirement for them to post on social media before, during, and after events to ensure maximum exposure for the company and its affiliation with them.

When you do post before an appearance or event, make it count. Don't just tell people what you're doing. An elected official with a bad impression of social media once grumbled to me, "Why do people post: 'I'm going shopping!!' Who cares?"

He's absolutely right that there is no reason for him to take an interest in the shopping habits of a random constituent. The same is true of a person he finds influential. If they just post: "I'm having a suit tailored and just bought a yellow tie," it's completely irrelevant and only serves to annoy the readers. Only relevant posts have the power to reinforce a brand.

If Suze Orman or Mark Cuban goes to a store with an innovative concept, like Everytable, posting about shopping has potential. Everytable is a grab-and-go store serving fresh, healthy food at economical prices to address food deserts in low-income neighborhoods where there are a lack of farmers markets and healthy choices. Because their brands are built around finance and entrepreneurship, either one of them could easily turn an "I'm going shopping!" post into a stellar opportunity to promote social innovation in business.

The power of linking a post to your brand is strong enough that you can even get by with a personal photo occasionally.

Suppose you're a travel agent taking a vacation in Sri Lanka. You might post a gorgeous photo of palm trees leaning over the surf toward the sun with either of these remarks:

> Kicking back with cocktails at a spa on the beach in Sri Lanka. This is the Life!
> Flew 9,000 miles to check out the quality of spas in Sri Lanka, so you don't have to. What I go through for my customers!;)

The first one says you're having fun, which has no value for your brand. The second says you're looking out for your customers' interests and jokes that it's a chore to go to a spa in paradise.

If you meet a celebrity at an event and you post a photo with the both of you in the frame, the celebrity's image will undoubtedly get attention on its own, but if you want it to have any value for your brand, you need to make the connection explicit.

When an executive for a sustainable energy company runs into Elon Musk at the annual Consumer Electronics Show in Las Vegas, which of these posts is best for the company's brand?

> Wow! @ElonMusk showed up this year! #CES
> Up Close with @ElonMusk talking about lower emissions in self-driving cars. New ways to go Green! #CES

Don't expect your followers to figure it out. It's on you. If you post something that seems random, people may click Like anyway—out of courtesy or guilt—but those Likes aren't buy-in. They don't help you. You have to make it clear why they should care.

It's fine to tell people what you're doing, but let them know what it means. Simon Sinek, author of *Start with Why: How Great Leaders Inspire Everyone to Take Action*, has built an entire brand around the fact that "people don't buy *what* you do, they buy *why* you do it."

Your Images Matter

Visual content grabs much more attention than text on every platform. Scientists at MIT tell us that our brains can process an image in thirteen milliseconds (thirteen thousandths of a second!).[21] We are hardwired to recognize images more quickly than text. As you can see, when you post images instead of only text:

- Social media posts get 650 percent more responses.[22]
- Facebook posts get 87 percent of all engagements.[23]
- Tweets get 18 percent more clicks and 150 percent more retweets.[24]

Video does even better—attracting *three times* more engagement than text.[25]

The impact will be strong, so be sure you post only images that match and enhance your brand. It's not safe to assume that anything that interests you will interest your followers. And even if they do, you're not on social media to get Likes. Everything you post should be carefully crafted to support the message you are there to convey.

Images you post on social media should reflect who you are. If your image is polished, you should never post sloppy, poorly lit snaps. They may be fine for another market, but they don't match your brand.

When you are a real estate broker, promoting properties and keeping people aware of trends in the mortgage industry, why would you post a photo of yourself riding a Harley with your friends? It's an irrelevant distraction that detracts from your message. Arnold Schwarzenegger can get away with it—whether he's the governor of California or the Terminator—because it's perfectly in keeping with his brand.

Kseniya Durst, a makeup artist I follow, never posts a photo of herself without full makeup on. The image she wants to reflect is that of a bold artist with HD eyebrows and beautiful shades of lipstick. No matter what she's talking about in a post, every image makes you say, "Wow, I want to look like that!"

If I can't go to your social media page and quickly determine what your brand is, you've failed. Will I have to wade through photos of your day at the beach or your new puppy in a hat to a single photo about your brand? If so, you've lost me.

Every image you post should reinforce the perception that you are the go-to person in your niche. People now come to my page to find out what my take is on breaking news stories. They've heard my opinions before and they got something out of what I said, so now they want to know if I am going to weigh in on a particular issue.

It wasn't always that way. I'm sharing with you the benefit of my experience. When I first started out, I was less laser focused. Sometimes I posted photos on Instagram without taking time to edit them or asking myself whether they were just about me or had anything at all to do with my brand. That's what happens if you're not intentional.

My social media pages should scream "advocacy." Every time I post, I ask myself, "How do I tie this to my brand?" When I get an award, I never post about it without figuring out, "What's the point of this for my brand?" That's why my posts aren't just about me broadcasting that I received an award; rather, the posts say I'm thankful for the opportunity to raise awareness about women in business or special needs children. That's a branded post, the other is a selfless plug that may be fine for some, but not for rainmakers.

Years ago, when I was starting out on social media, a Los Angeles publicist, Monique Moss, gave me a scathing critique of my Facebook fan page because it was all over the place. Like most people, I posted anything that interested me. It felt like a conversation I might have with my friends. As a result, most of my followers were friends and family. That was nice, but it wasn't doing anything for my business or platform.

Monique said, "This is horrible. What do you stand for? What's your message? Looking at your social media accounts, I have no idea. If you want to jump on more news channels, where are your comments about breaking news stories? Why aren't you joining in on the social media conversations with news anchors? Why have a page if you're not using it to solidify your brand?"

She told me to do an audit and delete anything that did not directly reinforce my message. No more of the sweaty exercise photos I loved unless I was promoting running and healthy lifestyles for women or a cause that increased awareness of my brand.

I went through all my social media pages, culling anything that didn't fit. Now I'm extremely selective about what's on all of my pages and timelines. You'll see me getting awards, appearing backstage or on the set, featured in magazines, writing blogs, and hanging out with celebrities on red carpets at charity events, and even lots of running and exercise shots. What you won't see are photos of my kids' report cards or my latest vacation shots— unless they're related to my brand.

As for those sweaty running pictures I love to post, I realized that they are very much a part of my brand. They're also the posts my followers find the most inspirational. It wasn't that the pictures were wrong, it was the messaging and positioning. Tying everything to my brand still gives me a lot of latitude to post those sweaty exercise shots, but with a new on-brand message. As a result, I have had hundreds of people tell me that my running posts encouraged them to lose weight, change their eating habits and exercising routines, tackle projects they had given up on, and in one instance even run a half marathon!

It's about being conscious, having a story, and staying consistent with that story. Once I made these adjustments to sync my social media to my brand and to tell my story as a civil rights lawyer, TV talk show host, legal commentator, and autism advocate, I experienced significant growth in engaged followers, which led to more media appearances, influence, and opportunities.

The biggest mistake I see people make is not using their social media pages to promote their brand. That's fine for a personal page, where you gossip with your family and friends, but if you're not using social to set up a business page, you're missing one of the most exciting opportunities of our time to cultivate followers and magnify your exposure.

Be conscious about what you're posting. Don't post bad profile and cover photos. It still amazes me when I see blurry, dark, dingy photos that are downright unflattering. Why would a professional choose an image like that to present themselves? There are too many filters and apps that allow you to correct photos in a couple of minutes. Think about your image. What are you trying to project?

When to Post

Social media is *now*. It takes place in real time. A breaking story is old news twenty-four hours after it's been resolved. The Oscars is a good example of an event that is wondered about and written about for months, but whatever happens there quickly dies on the vine. Hopefully, the award winners get a career boost with a longer arc, but it's impossible to generate any interest in the jokes, the clothes, and even the faux pas by the following week.

Some articles and events, like I said earlier, are what we call evergreen. Home ownership will be relevant to people next week and next month. Recipes, child rearing, travel, the environment, cities, human interest stories, and many more topics will stay relevant year after year. Your appearance on a TV, web, or radio show will not. To get the most out of each appearance, you need at least three posts, timed strategically.

Before

Post to let people know that you're going on and attach it to an image. Maybe you post your message with a photo of the station's set or logo. Sometimes when I go to a set at 3:00 a.m., before sunrise, I take a photo of the dark street from inside my car on the way to the set. The more intriguing the photo is, the better.

You may tease your appearance by posting hours before and again before you go live. *The Doctors* routinely posts as early as 6:00 a.m. on the day of each show tagging the guests and hosts. I will then repost using a picture from the show or a link before the show airs. I follow the posts for engagement and will repost later after the show airs with "ICYMI" before the link. This lets my followers know that I posted the link earlier, but want to make sure everyone had a chance to see it. If it's a picture with the male exotic dance group, Thunder from Down Under, and a clip of them demonstrating dance moves that are guaranteed to help you stay in shape, I can count on lots of engagement and sharing across all platforms!

If you have been on the show before, post a great shot of you with the host, with the producer, or by yourself in the studio. It will remind people that you are a regular on the show and subtly remind people that you are in demand.

Stay on message no matter what. Maybe you're a former Olympic athlete being interviewed about the Games of the Century in your sport, or you're a disability rights expert talking about the Special Olympics. Whatever the reason is, it has to be consistent with your brand. If you're just telling your friends about it, you can say you're going on Channel 5 to discuss the upcoming Olympic Games with a famous sports commentator and leave it at that. But if you want to be a rainmaker, you've got to say more than that in posts that reach your prospective customers. Whatever your expertise, it's important to say more. Mention the follow-up chat you'll hold with your followers on Facebook Live to give insider details about your sport and your upcoming appearance or class or product. Name recognition is great, but you want to include the next way for your prospects to connect with you or learn more or take their engagement further.

Never post anything without asking yourself: How it this relevant to my brand? If you're being interviewed, make sure you know why you're talking to this person. How does the show or the interviewer relate to who you are and what you're all about?

During

Take people backstage with you. Make it real. "Now I am here on set with [anchor's name] of [name of show]." Always be sure to use specifics. So you'll name the anchor and the show. You'll let people know when the show is coming on the air. If it's a taped segment, you want to be sure to make it clear that you are on set taping a segment rather than appearing live.

I once had a producer take a picture of Michaela Pereira and me on HLN's morning news show. Minutes after leaving the studio, I posted the picture on Facebook, tagging her and the show. It got close to one thousand Likes and tons of engagement. Michaela is very popular and has a large following since she was a local anchor on a station in Los Angeles and a CNN morning show. Our respective audiences loved seeing us together discussing a matter they cared about.

If you tag an anchor, a radio host, a podcast host, or a journalist, always use a trending hashtag. Twitter lists the top ten trending hashtags. Hashtags.org lets you search for hashtags and provides a twenty-four-hour trend graph showing peaks in usage. You can also simply choose a hashtag already being used by the people you want to tag.

Trending hashtags give your post the ultimate leverage. If a meteorologist with eight hundred followers tags a TV anchor with a huge following and the anchor retweets it, that little post may go out to five hundred thousand people. If your tweet or post is not engaged by the anchor, don't despair. You have already sent a powerful message to your own audience, and if they share your post, you are getting rainmaker leverage and exposure.

After

It's all right to wait until the studio posts the file of your appearance on their website. Then you can repost that link. You don't have to do it the same day. But it will have the most relevance and benefit to you if posted as close in time to the event or the airing of the segment. Otherwise, your post may be completely overshadowed by the latest breaking news.

When you post the link, you might add:

> "I sat down yesterday with [anchor's name] to discuss [unique angle on this issue]."

Engage the audience by asking their opinion as often as you can. Rather than ending with a generic prod like "What do you think?" or "Click Like if you agree," it's far better to build your question into the topic.

Mark Hyman, MD, is a master of this. With more than five hundred thousand followers on Facebook alone and hundreds to thousands of Likes and comments on most of his posts, it's safe to say he's doing something right. Here are excerpts from a few follow-up posts that integrate the question with the topic:

> "Three recent studies add to an increasing body of evidence that saturated fat is not the evil, heart-disease-producing substance we once thought...Now I want to hear from you. Have you added saturated fat, like coconut oil or grass-fed butter back into your diet? How has it affected you?"[26]
>
> "Plants grown in the wild have strong defense mechanisms....When you eat wild plants, you ingest their ability to defend against stress. Isn't that incredible?"[27]
>
> "Are you still consuming dairy? If so, here are some facts to consider..."[28]

When you post the link to your appearance and ask the question, they're even more primed for engagement and far more likely to comment, instead of just clicking Like. When they do comment, be sure to answer. Don't let it be a one-sided conversation or a thread between your followers without you there. These are the people who want to know what you think. Don't relinquish your role as expert to others. Your followers may appreciate the comments from your other followers, but ultimately it's you who brought them to the page and will keep them there. When you chime in, they feel like they are actually sitting down with you over coffee. The connection is invaluable!

Build Your Tribe

If you market information of any kind, such as books you've written, social is ideal for engaging your readers directly. It offers opportunities that were never dreamed of by any previous generation of writers in history. You can build a tribe of followers from all around the world, who eagerly await your next book.

To get the most mileage out of your social media presence, always find new ways to encourage people to repost, to expand your following, and to connect with your most loyal followers directly. Social media is incredibly flexible. The only limit to these ideas is your own creativity.

Enormously popular pop culture blogger and author Luvvie Ajayi, who uses the moniker Awesomely Luvvie, engaged the five hundred thousand followers of her blog when she went on a national book tour to promote her *New York Times* best seller *I'm Judging You*. Eager followers stood in long lines and paid an entrance fee to hear the no-holds-barred author unleash her brand of social critique, and in return they went home with a copy of her book. She effectively uses her social media account to promote her book with clever tweets containing pictures of airport bookstores that carry the book. A couple of months after her book was released, she surprised her 145,000 Twitter followers with news that the book had been optioned by Shonda Rhimes, the award-winning writer and producer of *Grey's Anatomy* and *Scandal*, for a cable series.

Photos That Engage

As often as you can, get people involved. Think of it as a game—related to your brand—that you play with your followers.

British Airways 747 pilot Mark Vanhoenacker posted a photo from the cockpit while he was in flight, then he invited his followers to post photos taken from the windows of planes.

It wasn't a random connection to his profession as a pilot. It was closely linked to his brand and his critically acclaimed book, *Skyfaring: A Journey with a Pilot.*[29]

Process Videos

Even before you start appearing on shows, you can post personal videos demonstrating your knowledge, skills, and brand. For example, if your goal is to be a guest on major cooking shows as a celebrity chef, you can post videos showing your followers how to make your recipes, teach them chef skills, or take them with you to the farmers market to select the best produce.

Add an element of adventure by buying fish from fishermen at your local dock or exotic locales like the Greek islands. Introduce your audience to the artisans who make olive oil, bread, or wine. If fresh ingredients are a part of your brand, help them fall in love with those ingredients by showing them the difference in how they're produced.

Create Contests

It's fun and easy to run contests that challenge people to compete with each other while spreading your content.

Naming contests are popular on social media. Authors ask followers to vote on the titles of their chapters or offer to name a character after the winner. Contests can be run to name recipes, new products, services, events, awards, and almost anything conceivable.

Not all of the best marketing campaigns were produced with huge budgets and massive marketing teams. Viral campaigns that spread like wildfire across the Internet every single day were often started by small business owners who relied on ingenuity and an enthusiastic crowd.

Keep in mind that, while contests are legal in general, the

rules vary from state to state. Consult a business attorney to make sure that any online contest you run complies with the laws of the relevant state(s).

Trending Tags

A quick way to build a following on Twitter and get people you've never even met to retweet your content is to add a trending tag.

All you have to do is identify trending hashtags and jump into the conversation. People will see you, interact with your tweet, and follow you. I do it routinely for big events—political debates, the Grammys, the Oscars, women's marches.

On Twitter mobile apps, you can find trends by tapping the Search icon. On a computer, type "trending now" into Search. Or look at the influencers you follow to find trending hashtags in your niche.

Research Photos

When you post photos taken during your research, it's like taking your followers along with you. Not only does it give them a behind-the-scenes look at what you're developing, but it is an excellent way to boost engagement. Joanna Penn, a *New York Times* best-selling thriller writer, travels the world to do research for her thrillers.[30] On her website, she creates book pages with titles like "Behind the Scenes of My Book Research for *Gates of Hell* in Granada, Spain" (jfpenn.com/book-research-granada), then posts the links on social.

> On a recent trip to Granada, Spain, we visited the Alhambra which I use as a setting in *Gates of Hell*. In this short video, you can get a taste of the atmosphere at the Nasrid Palace along with some Spanish guitar

music (which I love!). Below the video, I have included an excerpt from the scene. You can also see all my pictures from the trip here.

Penn's page includes an excerpt from *Gates of Hell* illustrated with photos from Granada, a two-minute video of stills from her trip, a link to buy the book, and a limited time offer for a free copy of her novel *Day of the Vikings*—if you provide your e-mail address.

CHAPTER 9

Engage or Fail

I n an environment where social media users are notorious for posting back-to-back selfies, it may sound strange for me to tell you that people don't promote themselves enough. But I see it every day.

Time and time again, folks make the effort to get media appearances or show up at events filled with influencers, then completely fail to leverage those experiences to enhance their brands. In a rich media environment filled with exciting opportunities, they behave like Luddites, sticking fearfully with what they know, instead of mastering the most effective ways to promote their brand like rainmakers.

Talk shows and news programs need a constant supply of fascinating new guests. I've said it before and I hope you can hear me: There's never been a better time for you to use the media to amplify your message and be positioned as a go-to expert in your field.

It's heartbreaking sometimes to see so many people missing the boat on this one. As a rainmaker, you should always be thinking of how to leverage your appearances to get the most out of them.

When an ordinary expert goes on a show, that's basically the end of it. They may tell their family and closest friends, make sure to list the appearance on their website or CV, and even write a fake "humble" update on their personal Facebook account. But that's about it. The best outcome is that someone watching the show buys their book or the producers ask them back.

That's not going to cut it, if you want to make it rain.

Getting Leverage

Media appearances are your moment in the spotlight. For those few minutes, you are being watched by thousands or even millions of people. Assuming you're not already famous, almost all of them are new people who don't know you. So it's a thrilling opportunity to get your message out and create name recognition for your brand. But never forget: a media appearance is a stepping-stone, not an end goal.

Let's say you've been invited as a guest on *Good Morning America* to talk about a rock star inducted into the Rock & Roll Hall of Fame. You gave the producer a strong pitch with three great talking points and made it clear why you were the best person to bring on the show. Maybe you've written a book that positions you as an expert on this topic. Maybe you used to play in the same band when this rock star was just starting out. Whatever your connection, the pitch worked. They're delighted to have you.

For five glorious minutes, you're sitting in front of the cameras with perfect hair, clothes, and makeup, giving it all you've got. Because the hosts have your talking points, they set up each one with questions or comments of their own, and the interview is smooth sailing. The audience loves it, the producers are happy, and you come off the set on an adrenaline high.

Good Morning America often gets 5 million viewers. The good news is, they were all watching you for five minutes. The bad news is, it was five minutes out of a two-hour show seen by viewers who typically watch at least 4.5 hours of TV every day. You had great visibility 1.8 percent of that time. So you're not going to be able to post one update, then sit back and wait for your book to hit the best seller lists.

It's still an incredible opportunity that can utterly transform the way you do business. That's why I've written this book. Media appearances have the power to bring you a huge following of like-minded people who care about your book, your message, your products—but only if you leverage it right.

My own book publicist, Sandi Mendelson, an expert with thirty-five years' experience creating best sellers and building authors' brands, says, "A few years ago, one appearance on a single segment of a show with millions of viewers would make book sales go through the roof, but that isn't enough anymore." Now you have to amplify that appearance on as many channels as you can to maximize that value and bring people to your door.

It's harder now to gain superstar status, because there are so many media channels. With such a deluge of information, people naturally pick and choose what they follow. Viewing is much more fragmented than it was even a few years ago. In that noisy environment, the old sales adage about people needing to see an ad multiple times before they take action is heightened even more.

No one's ever agreed about how many times is optimal—probably because it varies. But maybe you'll recognize your own thought process in what Thomas Smith famously said about how people react when they see a new ad.

The first time, we don't even see it. By the fourth time, we have a fleeting sense that we've seen it somewhere before. It's not until the fifth time that we actually pay attention enough to read it. Then, of course, the next few times, we start to get annoyed by seeing it again ("Same damn ad!"). By the ninth time, the magic kicks in. We start to wonder if we're missing out on something.[1]

For Herbert Krugman, the number of exposures is less consistent than the three mental stages taking place:

- Curiosity ("What is it?")
- Recognition ("What of it?")
- Decision ("I want it.")[2]

The number of times it takes to get to a decision can vary from person to person on any given day, whether it's a decision to buy a book or check out an expert's website after seeing them on TV. The only indisputable fact is that people need to see you repeatedly before they take action.

Turning one media appearance into many exposures has never been easier. Social media allows you to instantly amplify a single event across multiple channels to quickly move people past "What is it?" and "What of it?" to active engagement with your brand.

A lot of the people I meet don't understand its astonishing capacity to raise their visibility by magnitudes. When my friend Debra opened a trendy new restaurant in Florida recently, I asked about her social media presence. "Oh, I've got a Facebook page, but that's it. Instagram is not my thing."

She was letting her personal thoughts about Instagram guide her business decisions. All she knew was that as a person, she'd never used that channel. She didn't think about why it might be critical to her business success. She was looking through the wrong lens.

Whether or not you feel personally drawn to the idea of social media is irrelevant. Did anyone who ever ran old-school business ads in newspapers ever feel a personal affection for print ads? What you feel personally isn't the point. It's simply a phenomenal business opportunity. My friend and social media consultant, Brian Ross Adams, says that one of the hardest concepts for people to grasp is "getting clients to recognize that promoting your business or brand on social media is business, not personal." Even his most sophisticated clients have to be constantly reminded.

Debra had no idea that there were scores of avid foodies on Instagram. She'd never seen the food porn photos that populate that channel around the clock. Instagram users love going to restaurants, raving about the food, taking photos of what they order to memorialize the presentation, then posting it with the name of the restaurant.

When you're a rainmaker, you see business opportunities where others see nothing at all. It's not to say that you ever need to develop a love for Instagram or any other channel in your personal life, but when it comes to your business, you want to make it rain!

That means asking yourself: What's going to give my brand the most visibility? Where else can I spread my message, share information, and connect with the people I want to influence? How can I make the best use of the amazing marketing channels I have at my fingertips? Am I missing any chances to expand my reach?

Just starting out with her first restaurant, Debra wasn't asking those questions. She hadn't made that important shift to thinking like a rainmaker.

Social Media Isn't Advertising

Social media is a two-way street. You're not advertising. You're not posting something for people to read passively like an ad on a bus. It's a conversation.

Maybe it sounds harsh, but let me be blunt: If you don't find a way to engage on social media, you will fail to make it rain.

You cannot build a meaningful platform where you influence your followers and get your message out without engagement. This may be the most difficult concept for most users of social media to grasp. A lot of people seem to think social media is a free billboard to boast about their latest accomplishments. Countless posts on Facebook, Twitter, and Instagram about everything from toned abs to paystubs leave you shaking your head trying to understand the point. It's hard to resist the impulse to say: "WTF?"

A few of these people are certifiable narcissists, but more often they're stuck in the past with an antiquated style that hampers rather than helps them build their brand.

Like a cocktail party, social media is interactive. If you don't *engage* people, it's like standing in the corner at the party, talking to yourself or giving someone the proverbial hand.

Whatever the medium, people are people. The same things catch their interest and get them engaged. If your social media pages are an endless stream of posts saying, "LOOK AT ME!!" you can expect exactly the same reaction as you'd get if you did that at a cocktail party. No one's interested. And just like a cocktail party, if you focus on yourself without regard for the people you're talking to, you are missing golden opportunities.

Great conversationalists realize that people often want the chance to express their own opinion or talk about an issue that relates to their own lives. It's only human. You may never meet your social media followers out in the world, but you need to treat them like real friends. Ask them what they think. Respond personally to their comments, like you would with a friend. This builds trust. Engage them and you will be rewarded with personal connections to your message. Not only will you end up with loyal customers who buy things, they'll sell them for you![3]

Do Your Part

Some celebrities have a million followers but zero engagement. Only a few people make comments or share. Even with the numbers, they're not an influencer if their posts don't generate active engagement. If your ultimate goal is to attract endorsements or to monetize your social media, demonstrated engagement is crucial. We have all heard of Instagram and YouTube stars who have incredible reach and power to influence everything from purchasing decisions to political elections. What these influencers are able to do is move people to action.

Magic Johnson is a great example. In life, he is one of the most approachable high-profile persons you will ever meet, often taking considerable time to engage with his fans and sign autographs. Over time he's built a solid reputation for being authentic, accessible, and friendly. Because of his engagement, he's become more than a superstar athlete. He's an influencer. People not only like him, they trust him and follow him. He is often sought out by national and local elected officials for endorsements, since adding his name can mean hundreds of thousands of votes.

Nicki Minaj, an American rapper from Trinidad that I follow, launched her career with three mixtapes, and now she has 21 million Twitter followers. I was surprised to see how engaged she is with so much traffic. When people compliment her, she quotes their tweet and thanks them. She's very interactive with her fans, and in return they reward her with their loyalty by purchasing her music and coming to her defense whenever she is under attack by the media or her competitors in the hip-hop industry. Nicki's smiley-face-emoji response to an adoring follower takes her less than thirty seconds to post, but is one of those intangibles that is worth many millions. One small gesture can turn a follower into a Minaj ambassador for life.

Some people with a lot of followers don't ever respond to comments. In the early days of social, around 2004–2005, many social media consultants and advisors espoused a theory that celebrities and influencers needed to maintain their mystique and to do so, they should avoid all interaction on social media. This old-school mentality encouraged aloofness from stars. It was built on the assumptions that social media was just a new place to advertise, and big-name stars should dispense their attention very selectively to keep their value high. Those days are gone. Now it's all about engagement. And it makes sense.

Think about it. If you start a conversation with a friend, you naturally expect them to engage. It's simple reciprocity. Social media is no different, but there we call it engagement. To make it work, you've got to do your part.

The first criteria is to match your brand, but after that you can tweet and post about books you love, artists you adore, events you attend, and anything else that allows you to support and praise other people while staying true to your brand. Even that paystub post showing your salary hike may make sense if your brand relates to women's empowerment, smart money management, or workplace success. That post can easily be a motivator or evidence of an important point about not undervaluing yourself rather than a "LOOK AT ME! I make a lot of money!" which is not only obnoxious, but a big turnoff. Plain and simple: Don't make it all about you. That's a quick way to sabotage your brand and get people to unfollow you.

When you can, turn your posts into conversations. "Click Like if you AGREE!!" is not a conversation. Basic social skills are what you need to get a conversation going. So any extra training you take or books you read on making friends or starting conversations will improve your skill set for social media, too.

Social Media Skill Set

A lot of times people ask me about a TV interview I've done. They missed seeing it and want to know what happened. Maybe I was talking with Dr. Phil and his guests about a child custody case. So I post the link and ask them to weigh in on the issues. ("We discussed child visitation rights across state lines. What do you think? Do you side with the father or the mother?") When people start answering, getting into the conversation, I make more comments in response or say, "Thanks for weighing in" even if I don't agree with what they said.

Other times, I may post a photo taken from my early morning run and ask: "What's your health routine?"

These kinds of posts are great ways to engage your audience and to create conversations that can lead to more engagement with potential new followers. Often when I start a discussion on my page about a topic from a media appearance, my followers not only click Like and leave a comment, but they tag their friends and share the post. It expands your reach and exposure far beyond your own base of followers. Often other experts and influencers will join the conversation.

You know I've said that anytime you're going to make an appearance, you should be sure to post ahead of time to prime the pump and create a sense of anticipation. As I noted in the last chapter, studies consistently show that images and videos are far more effective in getting attention and creating engagement than just text. Even a radio or podcast appearance can be made visual by taking photos as you go.

Though videos are even better than photos, be sure to follow up after an appearance with something more than just a link to the interview. Here are a few suggestions on how you can offer further value to your followers with your follow-up:

- **Quotes.** Post the most memorable one-liners from a blog post or an article you've written or from a media appearance. (If you don't have any memorable one-liners, be sure to come up with them before future interviews as often as you can, so you can post them later!)
- **Q&A Follow-up.** After an appearance where the host has asked you an important question, post that question and your response.
- **Quick Summary.** Post a summary of your interview for people who missed it. Be sure to include a relevant photo!
- **In-Depth Post.** Add to what you said in the interview by giving more details or further insights in a follow-up post. If your comments are too long for a post, provide a link to your blog or a PDF on your website.
- **More Tips.** If you gave two tips on the air, give a few more on the same subject in your post.

It's such a great opportunity to bring your followers into your world, promote the host and the studio, and spread your message to a wider audience, yet I don't see a lot of people doing this.

Most people tweet that they're about to go on the air or they take a selfie, but a surprising number of people fail to post the link to the appearance afterward. The studio has every incentive to provide a link because you are literally promoting their show.

In some cases, you can even tag the hosts, the guests you appeared with, the producers, or the show itself, but be sure to use good judgment. Don't abuse it. If you tag people too often, they will block you.

Think Strategically

If you've made an appearance as an expert on a story and it's getting local or national attention, you can launch a more targeted campaign, sending out that clip to producers or generally tweeting to those networks. They are already following the story, and your tag is a way to ensure you're on their radar.

This strategy is especially valuable if you are reporting on the issue locally, but would like to go national. Tagging producers on a post that includes the footage of you speaking with authority about the issue on the local media will immediately be perceived as relevant, not just self-promotional. Because they are already engaged with the issue, it's no longer "LOOK AT ME!" Now it's a way of providing them with more information about a story they're covering.

If your interview happens to have been on their local affiliate station and you provided a unique angle or invaluable information that hasn't been covered on their national news, it could give you the leverage you've been waiting for to move to the national stage. Tag the producer with a quick note: "I just sat down with your local affiliate to talk about... Here's the link." And cross your fingers.

The strategy is a good one, whether or not they call you right away. I've posted links and tagged producers a dozen times before I've heard back from them, but when I did there was a sense of an ongoing conversation, even if we'd never spoken. It's the way social media works. Even when people don't respond right away, it doesn't mean they aren't listening. They may be waiting to see a consistent pattern of high-quality posts or to find the right opportunity to invite you on the air.

Too Cool for School

When people say they're busy, I get it. I'm busy, too. Sometimes on social media, I get hundreds of responses to a single post. Can I cancel meetings at my law office or tell Anderson Cooper I can't make it because I'm backlogged? No. But you can read the posts and answer selectively. You've got to spend enough time that you can be sure your followers understand your message and get who you are. Otherwise, what are you doing there?

If you are eighteen to thirty-four years old, you are probably social networking 3.8 hours or more every day. I top that number by several hours, since I've incorporated social media into almost everything I do as a professional. From promoting my media interviews to posting blogs on my webpage to tweeting breaking news, social media is ingrained in what I do every day.

You don't have to emulate me, but the reality is business owners, senior executives, and decision makers are among the most avid users of social media. And there's a reason for it. They follow the trends and know that Facebook has the greatest impact on customers' decisions about what to buy. Yet there are still executives and entrepreneurs who aren't using social media to amplify the message and reinforce their brand. The most common excuse I hear from executives is that they don't have any extra time in their busy schedule to commit to social media. They lament about the endless meetings, phone calls, and demands on their times. Staying socially engaged sounds like another burden. Hoping for a compromise, many try to delegate social media to consultants. And although some consultants do good work, completely delegating your social media to a third party leaves you out of the loop with your own followers.

Remember, the busiest people on the planet—presidents, first ladies, CEOs, and the like—find time to post. Are you really too busy?

Comedians on the circuit can get help writing the jokes in their routine, but then they have to take it on the road. No matter how many years' experience they've had, every comedian knows that the joke that sounds good on the laptop may totally fall flat with an audience. So even if they get an HBO special, they're going to test the jokes, again and again, with live audiences to see which ones fail and which ones are audience favorites. They don't hire a team of assistants to try out the jokes in clubs across the country, they do it themselves. It's the only way.

On social media you won't know what your followers respond to and what they don't, if you don't engage them yourself. You need your audience to help shape what you say and how you say it. They will help you find your voice and make subtle adjustments to it over the years to keep it fresh and in touch with the times. That kind of engagement will let you know the ways your message resonates with people best.

No one can predict 100 percent beforehand what's going to work and what isn't. If they could, the Hollywood studios would always produce hits. Actors would never star in flops. A lot of times I post things and the response isn't there. Even when I am part of stories on major TV networks—with dozens of savvy producers, hosts, guests, and crews producing the best segment they can—some generate very little engagement and others go viral. There's no way to know for sure, but you can improve your odds dramatically if you listen and follow where your audience takes you. This doesn't mean that you are enslaved to the whims of the day or that you must adjust your message every time someone criticizes your posts. If you are an influencer, you will have detractors. Be prepared for that.

Several years ago, I was appearing almost daily on various news shows on HLN and CNN during the high-profile police shooting cases of African-American men in New York, Florida, Missouri, and Illinois. These cases generated huge viewership for the networks and lots of controversy over the state of race relations and policing in America. It was common for me to get hundreds of posts on my various social media channels following my interviews. Most days the comments were from people who agreed with the positions I advanced during the interviews, but on a given day, I would receive an equal number of hate-filled, offensive comments. I don't think I've ever been called so many derogatory names by strangers in my life!

Initially, I spent time responding to the posts and trying to convince my detractors that their positions were unreasonable, but I quickly discovered that it was futile. There is no reasoning with hatred and bigotry. That's when I discovered the Block, Delete, and Report buttons available on most social media channels.

My social media accounts bore similarities to my law office, where I often invited media, clients, and others for debate and discussions. If those discussions became disrespectful or counterproductive, I would terminate them and wouldn't hesitate to politely show someone the door. The Delete and Block buttons allow you to do the same on social media.

You are running these accounts, and although the sites have some rules that govern use, you should set your own rules. If people follow you or accept your open invitation to engage on your pages, they must follow your rules. Don't hesitate to sever a relationship that fails to serve your purpose. Abusive behavior was never meant to be a part of social networking. Follow my simple rule: My accounts, my way.

Social media detractors cause some people to be uneasy about exposing information about their lives and points of view to massive virtual social communities. They fear they will be attacked for stating an opinion or speaking out on an issue. This isn't high school. You are not trying to win a popularity contest. As an influencer, you have valuable information to share. You have worked hard to develop a body of knowledge. You have honed your message. Not everyone will agree with it, but those are not the people you want to engage.

Think about conservative political pundits like Ann Coulter and Sean Hannity. Their brand is controversy. They can tap into a sizable audience and not worry about those who only want to argue.

When you stop thinking about the obstacles and focus on the tremendous opportunities of social networking, you may discover, as so many others have, that when you're talking about things that really matter to you, it stops feeling like "exposure" and starts feeling like you've found a wonderful community of like-minded people all around the world that you never knew were there.

Social media gives you a way of communicating with more people, more easily than ever before. Apart from the tremendous advantages of getting your message out, building your platform, and becoming a rainmaker, you may simply find, as I did, that you love it!

Why Likes Matter Less

Great engagement is beneficial to your own brand in so many ways, but it is also a metric used by social media sites and search engines when they determine how much visibility to give you. Your engagement levels also tell producers and bookers a story and help them make decisions about inviting you onto a show. You don't have to have enormous social media accounts before you start pitching media. But as your appearances grow, you clearly want to launch an aggressive social campaign.

In 2013, Facebook famously changed its News Feed algorithm. It began to make different choices about which posts to make available to which followers. Like a search engine, Facebook began to give some pages dramatically better placement than others.

Only a tiny percentage—no more than 4 percent—of your followers see your posts at any time. For every ten thousand fans, your updates will be seen by only three to four hundred people at most.[4]

In the early days of social media, popularity and influence were assessed on the basis of the number of followers and page Likes. Now Facebook bases its decisions on an array of factors that are increasingly complex. Likes significantly lost value once it became obvious to the decision makers at Facebook that hundreds of thousands or even millions of followers alone did not necessarily convert to better business or influence.[5]

At the end of 2013, the value of page Likes was reduced even further by the new Unfollow option that allows a person who has Liked a page to opt out of following it. On a page with fifty thousand Likes, only fifty people may actually be seeing the posts for that page.[6]

As they say, the numbers never lie. And Facebook's analytics reveal that the magic formula is:

LIKES + ENGAGEMENT

Visibility is now determined by how many people click Like, leave comments, play the video, and share the posts, among other things. These measures are critically important to the Facebook business model. Not only are the people with the most engagement the most influential, but engagement equals advertising dollars.[7]

What this means is that when you're assessing your own reach or trying to identify other influencers, it's better to look at the level of engagement than the number of followers or page Likes. As exciting as it is to magnify your number of page Likes, it doesn't necessarily mean your message is getting through. It all comes down to engagement.

The Right Kind of Engagement

Say you're a talented young musician working hard to build a following by traveling the world to play in as many clubs and concerts as you can. But that's not good enough for you. You want to do more. So as you make your way across the great cities of Europe, Asia, Australia, and back home to America, you take time out to play in the open air.

You choose the big squares, teaming with shopping tourists looking for entertainment. You lay out your colorful fliers and prop up your CDs, then you start to play. You know you'll get them, once they hear you—you're amazing. And sure enough, an awestruck crowd starts to form. Their enthusiasm is such a rush, it inspires you and takes your music to another level.

As a musician, that's what it's all about. On a business level, there's another game in play. In that game, you know you have to generate an engaged enough following to make the music pay off so you can keep playing for a living. Inspiration is priceless, but it won't pay the bills.

Right now they're loving every minute, clapping and dancing in the street. How can you make sure they'll stick around for more? By constantly looking for new ways to leverage their engagement. Wouldn't they like to feel this good tonight—with their friends? Invite them to the club where you're playing. Let them know about the songs you won't have time to play that they can find on your CD. Tell them how you're working on a great piece and you'd want to let them know when it comes out. Instead of holding out a hat for spare change, work the crowd with an iPad and collect e-mails to send everyone a free MP3 of your new song.

If you consistently provide authentic value and information people want, you're doing important things right, but these things alone won't build an engaged following. The most engagement comes from good communication between you and your audience or the people in your audience with each other. It profoundly changes the dynamic from a bunch of people who all clicked Like one day on a whim to a bonded group that grows quickly and organically.[8]

Calibration

A community of loyal followers with a high level of engagement will promote your personal brand or products for you. While they may come to social media because they heard you speak on the radio or saw your appearance on TV on a topic they care about, ongoing online conversations with you and others can exponentially magnify the value of every person engaged.

The luxury car manufacturer Audi has mastered the right kind of engagement with its customers. It not only uses social media to collect page Likes, but by getting to know what its followers want, it has learned how to drive traffic back to its other web properties.

Audi's Facebook page has very strong engagement. Single posts can accrue more than ten thousand likes with two hundred comments and five hundred shares. By asking and analyzing what its own followers prefer, the people at Audi know what won't work. People don't want to see "extras" or unrelated posts, no matter how charming. They come to the page for Audi content, and that's what they expect. Anything else is a distraction that can rapidly attract unlikes and unfollows despite their best hopes.[9]

Engagement can be enhanced dramatically by calibrating your posts and comments to what your followers respond to most with Likes and comments. Your own website analytics will show you which videos and links get the highest click-through rate (CTR). Jumping into the conversation and listening to what your community says is vital.

If anything, people are turning to social media more than ever to get their news, form their opinions, and make their choices about everything from buying a car to making a restaurant reservation to booking a vacation in a foreign country.

Facebook reviews of restaurants, movies, events, and products of all kinds are growing at four times the rate of other platforms online, such as TripAdvisor, Yelp, Citysearch, Foursquare—and even YellowPages and Google.[10] You may have already unwittingly participated in that trend yourself. When you are trying to decide between two restaurants for dinner, do you check them out on social media? If you see that one place has 2,500 page Likes and the other has twenty-five, where do you go for dinner?[11]

As many as 62 percent of users go to Facebook to find out about local businesses, and 80 percent are more likely to buy from a company if there are positive reviews on its Facebook page.[12] You may not hear that from these customers, but you can be sure that engaging your followers by specifically soliciting their responses and reviews can have a much broader reach than you may ever know.

If you take a more granular approach, you can also increase engagement by adjusting the frequency and timing of your posts, as well as reposting things that match your brand and are already generating a lot of attention.

Frequency

We all know the infamous rule of Facebook marketing: "No more than two posts a day!" According to *Forbes*, there is little disagreement about this rule—provided you have more than ten thousand followers. With a larger following, two posts a day is unquestionably the best way to maximize engagement. With a smaller following, two posts a day can result in *50 percent fewer* clicks per post! Your total number of clicks for the week will be higher than if you posted only once or twice a week, but the engagement per post is far less. On the other hand, posting once a week with a small following can double your clicks per post.[13] Keep in mind that if you use an app or other tool to automate the posts, Facebook will decrease the visibility of the posts. So it's better to primarily post for yourself.

After thirty minutes, half of the Facebook followers who will ever see the post have already seen it.[14] The post still circulates on Facebook for about ninety minutes, but after five hours it has reached 75 percent of its potential.[15]

On the other hand, frequent posting is essential on Twitter, which has an even shorter life cycle (twenty-four minutes). The ideal number of tweets depends on your goal. To increase engagement per tweet, one to five tweets a day is best. For more total responses, it's open season. Post as often as you'd like. When they disappear so fast, even fifty tweets a day isn't too much.[16]

Instagram is yet another story. Neil Patel of *Forbes* calls it "the weird kid on the social media playground." Establishing a pattern and sticking with it is the key to successful engagement on Instagram. Posting ten, twenty, or more times a day is fine. Just do it consistently.[17] People will adjust to your rhythm, but they'll lose interest if they can't depend on you to deliver.

Timing

Thanks to the marvel of analytics, we know exactly what works online and what doesn't—right down to the precise times of day that seem to be more effective than other times of day.

Results show that the days, frequency, and times below are likely to produce the most engagement. The times are local times—wherever your followers are online. So it may help to know that 50 percent of Americans are in Eastern time and 30 percent are in Central time.[18] If you are hoping to develop an international following, adjust your timing accordingly.

<u>FACEBOOK</u>
Days: Thursday / Friday
Frequency: 5–10 times/week
Times: 1:00 p.m. for the most shares; 3:00 p.m. for the most Likes

<u>TWITTER</u>
Days: Every day is ideal. Alternatively: B2B Saturday and
 Sunday, B2C Wednesdays
Frequency: 3–5 tweets/day. Response drops off after that.
Times: 1:00 p.m. for the most retweets; 12:00 p.m. and 6:00
 p.m. for the highest CTR

This data can provide informed estimates to use in your
own experiments. Like anything, your results may vary. What's
important is to know that results have shown the frequency of
posts and time of day can make a measurable difference. After
that, it's up to you to test these variations with your own community. All anyone can do is predict, measure, and repeat.[19] Stay
alert. Watch the metrics. See what works for you.

Viral Leverage

Never post anything that does not enhance your brand, either
directly or indirectly. That said, one of the best ways to get instant
engagement is to post something that's just gone viral! Not yes-
terday. Today. Posting a meme that people are already sick of will
do you no favors. If you do see a viral meme that's current and
matches your brand, don't miss your chance.[20]

Think about these top viral videos and photo memes. What
kind of brand would you need to tie into them? What would you
say in the post?

Salt Bae. Nusret Gökçe, a Turkish restaurateur, posted a video
on Instagram showing him masterfully chopping and applying
shimmering salt to an Ottoman steak as if it were fairy dust. His
salting move is so distinctive, it's showed up everywhere—from
graffiti on the streets of Melbourne to a preening dance by soccer player Danny Welbeck in the UK when he scored two goals.[21]
As the image went viral, Gökçe used it to expand his restaurant
business in both Britain and the United States.[22] Although he can't

speak English, he says he hopes to "communicate with people through meat."[23]

In 2009, photographer Stephan Savoia took an iconic photo of Michael Jordan crying during his Hall of Fame induction speech. Little did he know it would become one of the greatest memes of all time, with an unusually long life.[24] Now Jordan's face is Photoshopped over the head of anyone who is moved to tears or suffers a defeat.

The result of the U.S. presidential election in November 2016 was so startling that dozens of comfort memes imagining conversations between outgoing president Barack Obama and his vice president, Joe Biden, filled the need for comic relief.

> BIDEN: "I left a Kenyan passport in your desk, just to mess
>   with him."
> OBAMA: "Joe..."
> BIDEN: "Oh, and a prayer rug in your bedroom. He's gonna
>   lose it!"
> OBAMA: "Dammit, Joe!"

Kayode Ewumi played a character named Roll Safe in his webseries, *Hood Documentary*. In the series, Roll smugly thought he had everything figured out, but he was all wrong. In February 2017, photos of Roll Safe tapping his head knowingly and making his remarks showed up on Black Twitter and went viral:

> "You won't be mad at me for being late if you stop thinking
>   I'm gonna be on time."
> "If I don't check my bank balance, I can't be broke."
> "You can't disappoint your family if you never made them
>   proud in the first place."[25]

On April 21, 2016, the day Prince died, Oscar and Grammy winner Jennifer Hudson came onstage with the Broadway cast of

The Color Purple after their show to sing a no-holds barred version of "Purple Rain" as a tribute. The audience joined in. The video of this event was quickly reposted millions of times.[26]

More than one video of James Corden has gone viral. Some say his Carpool Karaoke with Adele video was the number one viral video of 2016 with more than 152,000,000 views on his YouTube channel alone. Corden's videos of himself singing Stevie Wonder's "Signed, Sealed, Delivered" and other songs with Michelle Obama received more than 54 million views.[27]

Nusret Gökçe, James Corden, and the *Color Purple* producers made their own videos, which were reposted by millions. Often viral photographs and memes take on a life of their own, regardless of what the photographers or the people in the photos had in mind.

As you think about ways to get your own community to engage in conversation with you, be alert to the constant opportunities to join the conversations they're already having. Viral videos and memes are in that conversation by nature. Be on the lookout for the ones that match your brand.

Your goal is to become deeply embedded in your community. As you get to know your followers better, you'll find countless ways to engage them. Social media opens the door to connections with influencers in every realm of life. It has taken networking and promotion to an entirely new stratosphere. Even if you've been reluctant to participate before or didn't fully understand its potential, now is the time to start engaging on social media. It's not too late. And believe me, you don't want to miss it!

Diamonds in the Grass

You'd be amazed how often I meet people who have been in business long enough to make a real splash, yet haven't even considered learning how to amplify their efforts on social media. It's like leaving diamonds shimmering on the grass. All they have to do is pick it up.

When I cohosted an episode of *The Doctors* last year, one of our guests was a Harvard graduate and attorney promoting his new book. He made some insightful comments and did so well with the audience that I looked him up afterward on Twitter, thinking I'd follow him and tweet some friendly congratulations to help boost his appearance on the show.

What I saw there surprised me. I expected to be joining his conversation with his followers about the issues he'd weighed in on or how he'd enjoyed being on the air. Instead, I saw he'd done nothing to promote his appearance. There were no tweets at all about *The Doctors*, no conversation underway about his talking points on the issues nor even his upcoming book tour! Since he had fewer than two thousand followers, I assumed he'd only recently gotten on Twitter to promote his book.

This incredibly interesting guest had made almost *zero* effort to lay the groundwork for his appearance on a major nationally syndicated TV show. I was flabbergasted. But it got worse. According to his bio, he'd also been featured on CNN, MSNBC, and in a dozen major magazines—while doing next to nothing to amplify those opportunities far and wide on social media to build his following.

It's even more remarkable when you consider how easy it is. How long does it take to write a 140-character tweet or snap a photo?

He was in the studio with me at a show I cohost on a regular basis. We both went to Harvard. He could've asked me to pose for a photo with him on that connection alone. He missed that chance and this one, too: I was happy to boost his visibility on Twitter until I saw that he was not engaging his audience and getting in the game. His lack of effort made me lose my motivation to share a post that would've crossed over to my audience and introduced him to the hundreds of thousands of people who follow me. We have all heard it before and it's true: No one is going to do your work for you. But when you do it, others will follow.

It's like the pretty blond guest who came on *Dr. Drew* to talk about breaking news. I found her after the show, taking glamour shots of herself in front of *Dr. Drew*'s sign. When I walked by, she practically snapped at me to get out of the way! Wouldn't it have been smarter for her to say, "Hello, Areva. I see you're on the show regularly. Can we take a photo together? You must have a huge social media following."

What neither of these guests realized is that shows love guests who go on social media to promote their appearances. Some shows all but mandate that guests post photos and links to their appearances as a part of the agreement to come on the show. Producers know that when guests and hosts share posts, it amplifies the reach of the show even further. It's just good business.

Don't make the same mistakes these people did. See every media appearance as an opportunity to connect with more people. These environments are rich with connections. Will you approach it like a high school kid sucking up a chance to post a selfie? Or are you going to be a rainmaker?

PART V

MONETIZE IT

CHAPTER 10

Wield Your Connections

There is no such thing as a 'self-made' man," Yale historian George Burton Adams reportedly said. "We are made up of thousands of others. Everyone who has ever done a kind deed for us, or spoken one word of encouragement to us, has entered into the make-up of our character and of our thoughts, as well as our success."

In the rush to capitalize on opportunities, connect with everyone we can, grow our businesses, leverage our influence and influencers at every turn, we can forget the basic truth: a widening circle of influence is about genuine connection.

People will never come to trust you and respect what you have to say if they sense you see them as a means to an end. A classic narcissist uses people as what psychologists call "narcissistic supplies" and discards them without a second thought when they cease to be useful. Some people see networking as a similar kind of exploitation.

For rainmakers, networking adds value to their business through a continual dance of give-and-take. In many cases, real friendships form and business contacts become people who really matter, regardless of their benefit to your bottom line. Those connections will provide you with an ever-growing circle of people who recommend you to others because they've seen your work, your strength, your sense of purpose, your reliability over time, and they believe in you.

Now that I've established myself as an expert, most of the bookings I get these days come from producers and bookers I've worked with on shows dating back to my early days on *Dr. Phil*. Any time I'm on a show, I always make it a point to get to know and engage the producers. I try to make their jobs easier by being a good source of information and providing more than what's asked of me on a story or segment. In return, as those producers and bookers move on to new positions, I am often the first person they call on their new show. From cable news to daytime syndicated shows, I can now count on booking shows with producers I have worked with. I have even been a part of major TV pilots where I've met cameramen, associate producers, and high-level executives who are willing to vouch for me. This is networking that truly adds value.

This type of networking is not based on glib conversation at a cocktail party and exchanging cards. It's not a face-to-face pitch: "Hi, Rhonda, let me tell you something I'm doing that you might be interested in. Have you considered this topic as a segment for your show? I've got something to share that your listeners might be interested in." This is way beyond that.

When you make a real connection, you engage people and cultivate ongoing relationships with them. This isn't something you casually come to. You have to make a conscious decision to create an enriching circle of trusted relationships. You have to study the culture of the environment and adapt. You can't have your own, selfish agenda. It will never work. The ability to meet interesting people who will benefit your life as you benefit theirs is 100 percent intentional.

To do it right takes planning and preparation. You've got to get out there in the mix and stay engaged to make it work. As they say, nobody becomes an astronaut by accident.[1] But setting out to make great connections is not the same as setting out to exploit people. The only people who will warm to that are the ones who'll do the same thing to you. Those aren't the people you want to get to know better.

Not everyone you approach will respond as you hope. Everyone has stories of failed attempts to make connections. Don't let that hold you back. It's par for the course. In the end, the more valuable connections you make, the more opportunities will come your way at critical moments.[2]

My friend Eric Guster is a legal expert who has appeared on top cable shows on Fox News for some time. His appearances have helped his law practice tremendously. Every time he appears, he gets new clients. But he'd like to move to bigger shows with bigger audiences on major networks.

One way to make that transition is to leverage a local appearance into a national one. Because Eric's presentation in the interviews is every bit as polished and professional as it needs to be on a national show, the footage from local appearances gives him several options.

Let's say there's a police incident involving body cameras that hits the media. Since the Ferguson protests in 2014, police chiefs, lawmakers, and watchdog groups have encouraged the use of body cameras without necessarily thinking through the legal issues.

When the major networks call in experts, they bring talking points about privacy versus security, the dramatic increase in usage of body cameras by police departments since Ferguson, and their built-in limitations. Maybe one network brings on the head of the police department in the area where the incident occurred to give insight into the way the data from the cameras is secured and processed to protect the rights of citizens. The coverage is good, and because of further developments, the story continues to stay in the news.

Suppose that when Eric appears on a local cable show to

discuss the incident, he brings talking points with a unique angle that the major networks haven't covered. Maybe he points out that the regulations about the use of body cameras vary widely by jurisdiction. Further, he explains that Taser International, now called Axon, has an inordinate share of the market, producing 75 percent of all police body cameras. This raises concerns that Axon is exerting an undue influence on policing itself.[3]

After his interview, Eric waits for the footage to appear on the website for the local cable show, then posts it to social, tagging the producers of the major network shows covering the story.

> Just sat down with [news anchor's name] to talk about the body cam incident. 75% of police cams made by one company: Axon. Are they exerting undue police influence?

I always make a practice of this strategy to keep producers informed and let them know I'm weighing in on the issues, whether I'm on their show or not. Tagging can backfire if it's done too frequently and without merit, but done well it can help build your credibility with producers and, when the right circumstances converge, get you on their show. Even if they pick up the ball and run with it, using your talking points without inviting you on the air this time, you have provided a useful new angle for the producer. I'll say it again: The more you can make life easy for producers and represent a valuable resource, the more likely they are to think of you when they need an expert who always brings unique, well-informed insights.

Relationship calls are priceless. They can only emerge out of connections that you cultivate. As Keith Ferrazzi says in *Never Eat Alone: And Other Secrets to Success, One Relationship at a Time*, "The great myth of 'networking' is that you start reaching out to others only when you need something like a job. In reality, people who have the largest circle of contacts, mentors, and friends know that you must reach out to others long before you need anything at all." The secret is to find ways to make other people more successful. If you work hard to give more than you get, you'll achieve more than you ever dreamed possible.[4]

Eric is in an ideal position to do that, since he's been putting himself out there and making regular appearances for a while now. Considering the way media professionals move around, it's likely that some of them have moved up, too, going to work at CBS or NBC. They know he's good, competent, and capable. If one of his former producers at Fox News on cable is now booking appearances at NBC, it's obviously much easier for him to get an invitation, if he stays in contact and lets them know what he's doing.

Before, During, and After

As a media-savvy expert, you move in an extraordinary environment. Whether you appear on a local radio station or on major network shows, you are surrounded by prospective media connections who are perfectly aligned with your goals. Here's how to get the most out of every appearance:

Before

Apart from the preparation you'll do for your pitch and media interview, never make an appearance on a show without doing contact preparation.

Anchors and producers affiliated with shows that match your brand can turn into wonderful connections. Before you appear on the show, friend them, follow them, and set alerts for their social media accounts. These are people you want to know better.

As Keith Ferrazzi, author of *Never Eat Alone*, says, "Whom you meet, how you meet them, and what they think of you afterward should not be left to chance."

Although you'll be able to meet unexpected people on the

set as well, you can easily find out who a handful of people are beforehand. Do your research. Find out what they value and where they're coming from. Don't just look for business details. Try to get a feel for what they're like as a person. What do they feel strongly about? Of all the achievements in their bio, which ones make them feel the most proud? What's been going on with them lately—a new show, a difficult season, a move to a new city?

You're not going for doe-eyed stalker, just looking for enough information to be able to talk knowledgeably about their concerns when you get a chance to meet them. For a public figure, it will be flattering, but not surprising if you've been following their career. With a person who has a less high profile, it can create a level of comfort, as if you'd heard a little more about them through a mutual friend. In many cases, you may find common interests or backgrounds that you would never have been able to mention if you didn't do the research.

During

What many people don't realize is that employment in the media industry is in a constant state of flux. Hosts, producers, and everyone else on the staff may move to another network when a show ends or gets a revamp after the ratings drop. Over the years, you may find the people you met during a single media appearance all over the place.

Even a radically short version of Katie Couric's career makes a prime example. She started out as an assignment editor on CNN, then became a political correspondent on *Today*. She also coanchored *Now with Tom Brokaw and Katie Couric*. Years later, she joined *CBS Evening News* and *60 Minutes*, but still made appearances with her colleagues Tom Brokaw and Brian Williams, on ABC's *Good Morning America*.

By 2011 she had signed a $40 million contract to host *Katie*, a daytime talk show syndicated by Disney-ABC. With her own show, she immediately brought on former colleagues and connections she'd made on other shows, such as Christiane Amanpour, Diane Sawyer, Brian Ross, Richard Besser, Whoopi Goldberg, Michael Strahan, and many others.

When the show was canceled two years later for low ratings, she moved to Yahoo! News before the last episodes of *Katie* had even aired. By 2015 Yahoo! News formed a partnership that allowed her to loop back around to ABC's *Good Morning America* as a regular contributor.

Undoubtedly, every time she moved from one station to the next, one show to the next, she continually encountered producers, directors, writers, set designers, makeup artists, stage managers, boom operators, gaffers, grips, and editors who had worked with her on other shows. With constant turnover in the industry, it's inevitable.

After HLN's *Dr. Drew* show was canceled, several of the producers moved to new shows and networks. Several of them remember the work I did on Drew's show and frequently call me for segments. Producers at *Good Morning Britain* who see me on CNN frequently invite me to appear on their show. A producer I met years ago on *Swift Justice with Nancy Grace* was the segment producer on the *T. D. Jakes Show* when I appeared to give legal advice on several stories. Nkechi Nneji, who reached out to me to appear on Al Jazeera after following me on social media, moved to *All In with Chris Hayes*. Once she started her new position, she also reached out to me for appearances on MSNBC. Many of the relationships I have developed with producers have resulted in us working together on pilots for new shows and content.

Networking effectively while you're on the set is partly about being authentic. A style of engagement that works for one person will not always work for another. If you have a talent for chatting people up in a natural, easygoing way, by all means, look for opportunities to let that talent shine. If your style is more low-key, you can work that very effectively, too. Not all producers and hosts are alike. You'll soon be able to find those who are the best fit.

Two things you can do when networking on set are: thank the producer for inviting you; and begin a personal connection that you can cultivate later with at least three people on the set, whether they are producers, hosts, fellow guests, or others.

After

Always approach producers with great care. They are likely to be the busiest and most preoccupied people you will ever meet in your professional career. Whether you contact them on set after the show or later, keep it brief. You might ask them if they would be interested in hearing about any related experience you have that they may be unaware of. Let them know what added value you can provide. Just be respectful of their time and the fact that they are getting hundreds of pitches. Strive to stand out, not because you are the loudest or send the most e-mails, but because you show up, deliver a quality product, check your ego at the door, and stay persistent without being annoying. Professionals respect other professionals. No one respects a pest or a stalker!

Remember, the producer's job is to tell a story and provide information. They have to fill hundreds of hours with interesting content, week after week. Remember, whenever you can make their job easier, go out of your way to do it. Along the way, if you build good rapport and they come to rely on you, strong connections may forge.

The common wisdom is that in order to create recognition with a very busy professional, they need to see or hear your name at least three different ways—for instance, social media, e-mail, and face-to-face—before a new relationship can begin. After you've got some initial recognition, it's a good idea to nurture the relationship as often as once a month. With more peripheral relationships, two to three pings a year will suffice.[5]

Generosity

When it's working best, connection, like friendship, is a seamless process of continually giving and receiving. You make contact with valuable new people, then put those people in contact with one another. As you share your time and expertise with them freely, the pie gets bigger for everyone. The power of generosity is not yet fully appreciated.[6]

When you help more people, you find there's more help available for you. It's like a new app. The more people use it, the sooner the kinks get worked out, the more money the developers have for improvements, the more suggestions for improvements they get from their users, and the better the app becomes for everybody.

Don't keep score. It's not like that. Just make a determined effort to meet people who may be great connections and bring a spirit of generosity.[7]

Resources

TV producers, podcast interviewers, radio hosts, bloggers, social media stars—everyone is interested in great content. If you come across a story, even if you're not connected to it as an expert, send it on. Let them know that you're a valuable resource, too. I do it all the time.

Maybe you know that a producer is covering a story of an amazing surgery being performed on a child for the first time in the United States. You're not a medical expert, but you know the family. What's more, you've been following this producer long enough to know the kind of angle she likes. So you send her a message and let her know that you can help get an interview of the parents. It's not something the producer will soon forget. You've given her real value.

I once offered to be an expert on *Good Morning America* during the holiday week between Christmas and New Year's, when the regular legal expert was on vacation. Even though it meant going to the studio in the cold every day at 3:00 a.m., I was happy to pinch-hit. It gave me an experience that was not only invaluable but delightful, and an opportunity to demonstrate my worth to the show's producers.

Your willingness to go above and beyond is one thing producers will always remember. I am not suggesting that you devalue yourself or do things that offer no value to you, but remember that much of the work you do in the early stages won't pay huge dividends immediately. That doesn't matter because long-term relationships are far more valuable and important. Nurture them and they will pay huge dividends.

After so many appearances on the *Dr. Phil* show, I came to develop a great relationship with Dr. Phil; his son, executive producer Jay McGraw; his wife, beauty product maven Robin McGraw; and the entire McGraw production team. I learned the culture of the organization, and I was quickly adopted as one of the family. I am grateful for the tremendous opportunities they have given me. Dr. Phil and Jay gave me invaluable advice in the early days about how to make good daytime TV and never do anything beneath my brand.

Since then Jay and I have worked on many projects. Jay has been extremely successful in launching and selling shows to cable and networks. When Jay had the idea of a daytime talk show featuring attorneys that was similar to his Emmy award-winning show *The Doctors*, he cast me as one of five attorneys for the show. The show never aired, but we remained in contact.

Several years later, in 2016, I was doing small segments on the *The Doctors* as a legal expert, but I wanted to play a bigger role on the show. After I sat down with Jay to discuss the possibility, I became a recurring guest cohost on the show. I highly value my ongoing relationships with Jay, Dr. Phil, and the entire McGraw team. Creating mutually reciprocal relationships with producers and production companies not only makes sense, but is the mark of a rainmaker!

Free Books and Content

It may seem counterintuitive, but generosity can have a more powerful impact on your bottom line. When renowned author and National Book Award winner Neil Gaiman discovered that his book *American Gods* was being pirated in Russia, he was horrified at first. He worried that if he didn't fight to stop it, he would lose his rights to his own work. But then he noticed a strange thing happening in Russia.[8]

The more his book was pirated there, the more his sales went up, too. A whole new audience was discovering him through pirated books, then sharing the book with more and more of their friends. Although he's an icon in the UK, Gaiman was almost completely unknown in Russia. And yet the book was doing incredibly well there—thanks to the pirates introducing his book to an entirely new group of readers!

Never one to argue with success, Gaiman contacted his publisher. It took a lot of effort to persuade them to release a free digital copy of *American Gods* in Russia, but when they did, sales went up by 300 percent.[9] After thirty days, when the price returned to normal, the sales continued to rise. It was never about the price. It was about introducing him to the audience. Once they discovered his work, they loved it.

Now Gaiman simply thinks of it as people lending books to their friends:

> You can't look on that as a lost sale.... What you're actually doing is advertising. You're reaching more people. You're raising awareness.... Because the biggest thing the web was doing is allowing people to hear

things, allowing people to read things, allowing people to see things they might never have otherwise seen. And I think, basically, that's an incredibly good thing.[10]

Since Gaiman's early experiment, the advent of free content has blown the hinges off the old models. The expectations have changed. With so many brands competing for the attention of consumers, a simple promotion of a good product or service isn't enough any more. It's become essential to establish a level of trust before people are willing to buy a product or service.

When Amelia Lee started the Undercover Architect to educate, assist, and empower people who were remodeling their homes, she began with layers and layers of free content. A free e-book entitled *The 5 Biggest Mistakes People Make When Remodeling* was followed by a free checklist, a free webinar, and six useful, actionable e-mails over six weeks, before offering a training program for $99, then an advanced six-month course for $990, and an ongoing subscription to her popular podcast, *Get It Right*.[11] Today she helps more than five thousand homeowners a week plan their future homes.[12]

Like free media appearances, free books and content are invaluable ways to let people know how much you have to offer. Getting your message across with media interviews and great content is the best way to build a loyal following that raises your level of influence.

Your Specialty

If you have a huge social media following, you can make a connection with someone else in your niche whose target market is the same as yours and offer to promote each other on social media. The reality is that, if they have three hundred thousand followers and you have three thousand, it's not a fair trade. It will be hard to get them motivated, when the exchange is so imbalanced.

I often engage other influencers on social even without a formal reciprocal agreement. When the renowned ballerina Misty Copeland held a book event at a local book store in Los Angeles to launch her new book, *Ballerina Body*, I didn't hesitate to tweet out and post on Instagram a picture of Misty and me embracing at the event and encouraging my followers to go out and purchase her book. I not only admire her, but I respect how she has motivated a generation of dancers, particularly those on the autism spectrum. Engaging on social media was a way to help a fellow author, but also to connect with a new audience of dance enthusiasts and to motivate others to dream big.

There is a lot you can offer as well to foster meaningful relationships with influencers. Suppose you're a talented baker. Why not offer to give a free baking demonstration at an influencer's event? Afterward, they may agree to do a short three-minute video interview for you to post about how great the demonstration was. Keep it very organic. You could offer to cater a private meal at their house, then do a quick chat on Facebook Live while you're there.

> I'm sitting here with [your name]. She's just brought over her amazing cheddar cheese onion bread, fresh from the oven. I'm tasting it now.... Hey, this is good. I like it!

Whatever your specialty is, give away a sample for free. There's no question it will work; it's worked for thousands of years. People love to get something amazing for free. If you're a fitness trainer, you can go by their office and do a demonstration or offer them a free DVD of your latest program. If you're a chiropractor, you can give them a free adjustment. If you're a teacher, you can record a video to give away the first class for free.

This isn't about undervaluing your services or your worth. I am a strong believer in the saying "Know your worth and add taxes." This is value-added networking. You are not going to be offering free services to random people who neither appreciate you nor can reciprocate, either short- or long-term. You are strategically identifying people who have the ability to help you amplify your brand and whom you can assist in return. Your instincts and experiences will tell you if you are being taken advantage of or if the relationship has no value.

It's customary for lawyers to offer a free thirty-minute consultation to prospective clients. After all, hiring an attorney to handle an important legal issue is a significant decision that should be made with extreme care and vetting. I have formed hundreds of successful client relationships that have resulted in huge fees to my law firm that started with thirty and sometimes sixty minutes or more of free consultation.

As I became a more media-savvy attorney, I have also provided free legal advice to producers on shows that I didn't appear on. By making myself available and a resource, I have been able to parlay those relationships into regular appearances on some of the top-rated daytime and cable shows. This is the power of rainmaking.

Rewards

As you know from your own experience, the personal connections you make often bring far more joy and satisfaction to your life in the long run than any professional rewards.

One of the most famous connectors in American history was Katharine Graham, publisher of the *Washington Post*. Even though she published the Pentagon Papers and launched the Watergate investigation that brought down Richard Nixon's administration, Graham became close friends with Henry Kissinger. They used to go to the movies together. At her funeral, he was the first speaker to offer a eulogy.

Graham made connection a way of life. She cultivated trust

by making it a policy to trust others, expressing generously, and making it clear she had their best interests at heart.[13]

Referrals

Once you begin to form real connections with the people you meet in media appearances or even on social media, referrals can happen very naturally.

At this point, I get calls all the time to appear on shows in the United States and the UK. When I am unable to do a show because of contractual issues, scheduling, or other reasons, I refer them to friends or contacts I've made with other experts. I was unavailable to do live coverage on election night for the presidential election in New York for *Good Morning Britain*, so I recommended Eric Guster, the attorney I mentioned earlier in the book. Though he works in Alabama, he travels frequently to New York to appear on Fox News. Eric is looking to expand his appearances to other networks, and from his social media posts, the referral paid big dividends for him, as he is now regularly appearing on the UK network.

It's great for me to have someone reliable whom I can refer to producers. It strengthens my relationship with them, lets them know I am a trusted and reliable resource, helps them quickly fill a slot for a segment, and creates more opportunities for experts and professionals whom I work with regularly. There are no expectations on my part, but I am certain that the producer and the expert who gets the referral will remember the gesture.

Joint Pitches

By making strong connections with other experts, you can literally double your media appearances. When I'm asked to appear as a legal expert to comment on breaking news, I'm often paired with other experts on the show: psychologists, law enforcement

officers, FBI agents, social workers, and a range of other professionals. We bring our unique expertise to a story, lending insights
and opinions from our own perspectives.

Look for ways to create unique segments or exchanges with
other experts. When Dr. Drew had his HLN show, he frequently
covered breaking news stories like viral videos of police officers
involved in questionable conduct. John Cardillo, a former New
York police officer, became a regular voice supporting police. He
and I often disagreed on stories and were both willing to engage in
spirited, opinionated debates consistent with the style of the show.
These segments quickly became popular with the show's producers and generated tons of social media.

Once you've made a connection, you can consider pooling
your resources and making a joint pitch to comment on similar
cases. You can also share video clips of highly engaged and successful appearances of you and other experts from other shows
with various producers. If they like the chemistry and interaction
of you and the other expert, booking you both for a show makes
their jobs easier. The combined clout you bring may help the pitch
succeed. It makes the producer's job a lot easier, and that's always
a good way to get invited back.

Lucky Breaks

In Los Angeles, hardly a week goes by that you don't run into
a celebrity. It may happen less often in New York, but it's not
unheard of. A lucky break can happen anywhere. You could be
at a Starbucks at the airport, waiting for a flight back home to
Omaha, when a celebrity headed to London or LA sits down at
the table next to you. What will you do to make a connection?

If you're a financial advisor and you meet Adele, take the selfie. Send it to your mom or post it for your friends on your personal page. But don't make it a post on your business page if it
doesn't connect to your brand in any way. Sure, Adele has a

massive pop culture audience and an incredible voice. If you take a selfie with her over frappuccinos at Starbucks, you will probably get a lot of Likes. But you will leave your followers confused. There's no brand story to tell. What does Adele have to do with financial advice? It takes your message off track and, as cool as the moment may have felt at the time, it ends up being clutter.

However, if your brand is in finance and one day you have a chance encounter with Suze Orman, one of the stars of *Shark Tank*, and you talk her into posing for a selfie with you, you can find many natural alignments. Suze Orman has a well-established community of folks who care about financial advice. If those people were to realize that you were going to offer the kind of advice they're looking for in your TV interview next week, it would give your following a powerful boost.

These opportunities are why it's so important to continually work to build an engaged social media following that aligns with your brand. You can't rush to post it on a social media account you haven't cultivated and expect the post to be productive. You can't get social in a day. If you haven't built a solid community on social media with a uniting interest in financial advice, you'll get a few Likes, but it won't create the kind of buzz you would've hoped for from a chance meeting with a financial superstar. Rainmakers aren't star-struck groupies, they are influencers who live by that famous saying: "Success is when preparation meets opportunity." When you get a unique opportunity, make sure you are prepared. If Suze Orman checks social media and can't find you or sees an account that's directed to your family and closest friends, that's the end of it. You basically missed your lucky break.

On the other hand, if you were at your best and struck up a friendly conversation with her, Suze Orman might have actually considered posting the photo herself out of friendliness and generosity. If she checks social media and sees an engaged account that stays on message and targets exactly the audience she engages with, too, even though you have a lot fewer followers than she does, she just may post it on her own social media anyway. If she does, you've grabbed the golden ring and made your own luck.

What Suze Orman and others who are savvy about connections know is that it's not just about sparkling with a fleeting glimmer. It's about sending a message.

I was invited to a Christmas party at the home of comedian and social activist D. L. Hughley. We posed for a photo together. When I posted it, the message was not:

> Hey, look I'm at the celebrity party at D.L.'s house and we are kicking it with George Lopez and other A-list comedians!!

Instead, as always, my first concern was to convey the message I care about and that D.L. shares: autism. He has a foundation working on social justice causes and has been outspoken about his adult son with autism. We had partnered on a Christmas toy drive to give away ten thousand toys to autistic kids. There is enormous overlap. That post was easy:

> Great to celebrate the holidays with D.L. and crew as we enter the home stretch in collecting 10,000 toys for kids with autism.

D.L. has more than 2.4 million followers on Facebook and nearly six hundred thousand very engaged Instagram followers, many who may not be aware of his work with autism. When our collective followers see my post, they think, "Oh, they're working together. What are you guys working on? Maybe I want to volunteer." A post like that steps back vanity posts and encourages active engagement with our brands.

Never underestimate the value of the connections you make. Everyone is working hard to create a platform so they can do even better work in the years to come. The most successful ones will be moving on and moving up. If you find ways to help them and they find ways to help you, you're all better off. Not only that, but this kind of give-and-take with friends and colleagues allows you to experience the world as a better place. It's not just about getting more airtime or making more money. If you do it right, you may find that you also inadvertently improve your sense of connection to the world.

CHAPTER 11

Watch It Rain

In the early days after I opened my law firm, I faced the same challenges that all entrepreneurs encounter. I had to attract top talent, create a quality product, develop human resources policies and other operational systems, and figure out how to get clients.

In those days, I relied on what I'd learned from my brief stint at a corporate Wall Street firm and from my colleagues about using a combination of networking, relationship building, and advertising. What they failed to tell me was how difficult it was to be a practicing lawyer, while managing a firm and attracting new business. They also failed to tell me that advertising was terribly expensive and would require me to carve out a significant part of my start-up budget for the most minimally effective marketing campaign.

As a younger lawyer and new business owner, I assumed my senior colleagues knew best and tried to make their advice work. I wrote checks for advertising in targeted publications. I attended conferences and networking events any chance I got. I kept at it, even when it meant our marketing expenditure was in the tens of thousands of dollars.

In the end I realized that while some of these marketing efforts were more successful than others, none had the impact of making media appearances.

Today I can go on one show and, on a light day, I'll get ten people contacting me wanting to hire me. Depending on the show, it can be north of twenty. While not all of these calls convert to actual clients, each one gives me the opportunity to connect with new prospects and introduce them to aspects of my work that they may have need of in the future.

The exposure alone has amplified my brand in a way that allows me to charge higher fees for my services, attract high-profile cases, and generate substantial fees for my practice. No longer does the firm have to sink major revenue into advertising. Instead, I have actually been offered attractive sums of money to promote products and help other entrepreneurs and businesses generate revenue!

Many of my friends who provide expert commentary in the media have seen their businesses and brands transformed. When they appear on a local or national show, they are deluged with people calling or e-mailing to say, "I loved you on that show" and asking to set up an appointment or make a reservation, to become a new client for whatever the business is. They also have seen their visibility increase and lead to new lines of business and opportunities. Eduardo Lucero, a fashion designer in LA who regularly appears on an array of Telemundo and Univision shows, is a prime example. He may be best known for providing riffs about red carpet fashion at awards shows from the Oscars to the Latin Grammys. Eduardo can vouch for the fact that those appearances were instrumental in a lucrative contract he recently landed to be the stylist for a movie with a major studio.

The fact is, when you make regular media appearances, you amplify your business, your platform, and your profits. Every moment you are on the air, you are showing your clients and prospects that you are better than the competition and they should hire you.

As Måns Ulvestam, cofounder of the podcast platform Acast, says, "Without revenue, it's not a company, it's a hobby."[1]

Think big. How much business would you need to bring in

to reduce your spending on traditional advertising? What kind
of business expansion could a targeted audience make possible?
What could you accomplish with a significant following on social
media? How can you use social media to amplify your chances of
media appearances, and use media appearances to explode your
social media following? As you build your following, what will
you do to monetize it?

Abandon the old-school thinking where the only way to make
money is to get paid a regular salary and the only way to build
your business is with advertising. Those days are gone. Craft a
plan where you pitch producers so you can go on the air, then
bring your viewers to your social media pages where you engage
them and expand your brand and business by leaps and bounds—
this is the best thinking today. And believe me, it works!

Never before in history have we had an opportunity like this.
Don't let the old ways slow you down when you can use media
appearances and social media to monetize your business like never
before. It's absolutely essential to make a mental shift to this new
model in our digitally connected world. Engaging a wider community and customer base is the key to driving your success.[2]

A New Way

The national edition of the *Wall Street Journal* has a circulation of
1,350,000. If you run a quarter-page ad once, it costs approximately
$67,300. Targeting the Western states, where the paper reaches
only 330,000 people, the same ad would cost about $16,500—
for one appearance. At this writing, a quarter-page display ad
in the *Los Angeles Times* costs $24,137. A full-page ad is almost
$100,000.[3] Even if you can afford to run those kinds of ads, the
circulation of the paper is only 750,000 during the week.

Wouldn't you be better off making a media appearance that
goes directly to your target market?

Way back in 2013 the number of podcasts on iTunes alone

crossed the 1 billion mark, and they've been growing ever since. Popular podcast networks have huge numbers of downloads. Check out the continually expanding Podcast One (200 podcasts) and Earwolf (5 million per month, 100 advertisers, 130 podcasts).[4,5] How many listeners do the podcasts for your niche have? How many of them could you enhance by bringing valuable information to the show?

As I keep saying, bigger isn't always better. When I make six appearances a week on major network shows, I'm reaching millions of viewers, but I also reach millions when I appear on local affiliates. And so can you. The average viewership for the evening news on ABC, CBS, NBC, and Fox affiliates is 22.8 million.[6]

If you make an appearance on a podcast or an affiliate, is it really you *giving* your time away for free? Or is it you *getting* the massive, targeted advertising your need for free?

And that's just the beginning. Thanks to the power of amplification, you can send out links to every appearance on podcasts, YouTube, Facebook Live, TV affiliates, or major network shows over so many channels on social media that the impact grows and grows.

Can you even imagine reposting your lone $16,600 newspaper ad? It's all wrong. It's old-school.

If you haven't done it already, this is the time to change your way of thinking. There are incredible new ways to get your message out, build your brand, and monetize your business that have a bigger reach than you could have ever imagined, even if you had ads in all of the major national and local print publications in the United States.

Whether you are trying to influence people to get involved with a social cause or buy your book or come to your restaurant, the more exposure you get, the more opportunity you have to build support around it and watch things grow.

Since the 2016 presidential elections, we've seen how many petitions sprung up online and garnered three hundred thousand signatures overnight. It's proven true again and again. If you want to maximize your media appearance, where you talked about the issues that concern you most, you need to speak out forcefully in that appearance, then amplify it online. That's where the people are.

One-fifth of Americans say they're online "almost constantly." Overall, 73 percent go online every day and 42 percent several times a day. Young adults go on more often—50 percent several times a day and 36 percent constantly.[7] And the numbers are growing. In the meantime, daily newspaper readership dropped from 64 percent in 2003 to 39 percent in 2014.[8]

Your media appearances now give you the option of reaching higher numbers of a more targeted audience with your message. It's an incredible opportunity to increase your visibility and build a major platform.

The key is to monetize your appearances so you don't fall into the trap of having thousands of followers but no revenue. It's easy to be famous but broke.

In her article "The Sad Economics of Being Famous on the Internet," Gaby Dunn writes: "Many famous social media stars are too visible to have 'real' jobs, but too broke not to." While they have successfully built a following, these online personalities have to grapple with the cognitive dissonance of having a lively comments section and an empty wallet.[9]

Creating a higher profile with media appearances and social media is not the endgame. The higher profile gives you a foot in the door. What you do with it is up to you.

In many cases, the financial rewards of your appearances will be immediate. If, like me and many of my friends in the media, you offer a service as an attorney, a political analyst, a restaurateur, or a fashion consultant, or you have any other expertise that makes people immediately think, "I need that. I'll call her," the crossover is fairly direct. As I've said, after a TV appearance, I frequently get inquiries from prospective new clients.

If you run a sports club, an online educational organization, or a summer camp volunteer program, the rewards can also be immediate. Your appearance gives you an opportunity to speak directly to the people who most want to know what you most want them to hear. Whether or not your primary business involves selling products such as mortgages, video games, or ergonomic furniture, you should develop products to offer your prospects. It is an ideal way to monetize your media appearances. Information products are often very closely tied to expertise. Consider developing books, videos, audio recordings, checklists, slides, and other products to offer your prospective new clients when they come to your site.

Even if you don't have a product or service, media appearances can help you build your career and support social causes. Every time you appear, your influence grows, which puts you in a better position to get a promotion or snag the plumb assignments at work.

My Harvard Law School classmate Paul Butler is a professor at Georgetown Law School and a former prosecutor for the U.S. Attorney's Office. His regular appearances on MSNBC as an expert on federal prosecution of government officials have elevated his visibility in ways that can be used to leverage his standing at the university. As a go-to expert for the top-rated cable news channel, he can leverage up to higher compensation, promotions within the university setting, book deals, and paid speaking engagements.

Revenue Streams

The benefits of increased influence are not just monetary. But the most entrepreneurial way to turn a media presence into profit is to create a variety of revenue streams. In 2016, the top twelve Internet celebrities earned an annual total of $70.5 million (a 23 percent increase over the previous year). They did not fit into any particular niche. A rapper, a baker, a gamer, and a toy collector prankster each made more than $5 million last year—because they figured out how to monetize their free appearances.[10,11]

Almost 25 percent of television commercials now feature a celebrity endorsement.[12] With a product endorsement deal, signing autographs, taking photos, or posting about an advertising campaign can be lucrative. Often the only criterion is the degree of influence you have with a large number of followers that you may have built without spending a dime.

Rosanna Pansino is giving the Food Channel a run for its money with her extremely popular YouTube baking show, *Nerdy Nummies*. The low level of entry (an $80 camera and baking supplies) allowed her to start her channel cheaply. She leveraged her visibility by adding a cookbook to her revenue stream. It sold more than 120,000 copies. In 2015 alone, she made $6 million.[13]

The biggest media stars make everything count. They can make a living—and then a fortune—because they monetize their videos with preroll advertisements and find sponsors to pay for episodes or series.[14] They appear on YouTube, podcasts, television, radio, sell merchandise, and book speaking engagements.

The top YouTube channel for several years running has been PewDiePie. In every video, Felix Arvid Ulf Kjellberg makes comments on video games for 50 million subscribers (a 20 percent increase from last year) and a $15 million paycheck. He developed a game for mobile phones and further monetized his media presence by writing a book, *This Book Loves You*, which quickly sold 112,000 copies.[15]

Book authors are in an ideal position to diversify. Combining media appearances with YouTube videos taken during your research, Facebook groups on the book's themes, crowdsourced book or chapter titles, advice related to the book on Twitter or Quora, and hashtag campaigns to get readers talking about the book theme are all ways to expand the conversation—with book sales, speeches, classes, and videos to monetize it on the other end.[16]

Comedian Lilly Singh, who earned $7.5 million in 2016, expanded her revenue by developing her own lip gloss. Others have turned their media presence into their own shows on Netflix or YouTube Red (the subscription tier of YouTube).[17]

Tyler Oakley initially developed a media presence because he saw YouTube as a "microphone for marginalized voices." Now he's signed a deal with Ellen DeGeneres's production company. He monetized his 8.1 million subscribers by doing a world tour, then publishing a *New York Times* best-selling book of personal essays.[18]

Raising your profile can make speaking—in a tour, a workshop, a class, a video, or a webinar—significantly more lucrative.

During the recession in 2008, the speaking circuit took a hit. Corporations started cutting back. Even big conventions were reluctant to pay a lot for speakers when people were struggling. They were afraid it would result in bad PR.[19]

According to the National Speakers Association, the average annual revenue for a speaker today is $177,000. Most speakers make $6,000 to $10,000 per speech and give about twenty speeches a year. Naturally, the speaker's fee is augmented by sales of books and CDs.[20]

Before I started making media appearances, I was one of those speakers who frequently spoke for free or for very little compensation. I couldn't even command the average $6,000 to $10,000 paid to most speakers. My regular media appearances changed that. Now I can confidently set my fee at $25,000 and can turn down offers that fall below the average.

Corporate sponsors can often be enlisted to cover the costs when you speak to organizations that may not be able to afford your fee. If your target market is bankers, for instance, a mortgage company, mutual fund, or office supply company may be willing to sponsor all or part of your speech. Think about which companies would benefit from greater exposure to your audience, then make a proposal to their public relations department.[21]

Chris Widener, who charges $20,000 per speech, collects e-mail addresses about ten minutes into his speeches so he can send people additional materials. About 20–35 percent of the audience buys his books after the speech. The product sales far exceed the speaker's fee. "I've spoken to 3,000 people and sold $140,000 in product after a speech," Widener says.[22]

Despite what you may have heard, e-mail isn't dead. Social media may have taken over certain aspects of our connections with others, but 91 percent of consumers still use e-mail every day.[23] E-mail has higher click-through rates and results in a higher return on investment than other channels.[24]

With a list exceeding 115,000, Michael Hyatt says: "I have literally built a multi-million-dollar business on the strength of my e-mail list. Ninety percent of my income comes from it. Even today, my e-mail list is still my number one business priority— and asset."[25]

The formula for a massive e-mail list, according to Kevan Lee of Buffer, is:

AMAZING CONTENT + CRYSTAL CLEAR CALLS TO ACTION

Converting a social media following into e-mail just takes a little creativity. Offer any one of these options on social media in exchange for your followers' e-mail addresses:

- **Content.** Linking social media to content on your website.
- **Contests.** Prizes for a random drawing (while abiding by state sweepstakes laws).[26]
- **Community.** Facebook groups, LinkedIn groups, and Google+ communities.
- **Classes.** Video classes.

- **Quizzes.** Here the prize is a final score or evaluation.
- **Surveys.** Creating greater engagement.

The most overlooked ways of building your e-mail list doesn't require social media tactics or website optimization. Why not simply collect e-mails at any events or appearances you make? It can be effective, but you have to do it thoughtfully to avoid annoying people.[27]

- Give away a useful handout and ask for e-mails from people who want to receive the next one.
- Exchange a free service at a conference or trade show for e-mail signup.
- Host an event that people sign-in for via e-mail.
- Offer tickets to a future demonstration, appearance, or activity via e-mail.

If you are collecting e-mails live, it's easiest to take an iPad with you to collect e-mail opt-ins.[28] A few of the most popular apps for e-mail address collection are:

- Leadsie
- OnSpotApp
- iLeads
- QuickTapSurvey

Having a massive e-mail list can be a game changer and give you rainmaker status. If you write a book, sell a product, launch a new restaurant, or market a new service, being able to tap into thousands of people who have already identified themselves as interested in you and your brand is invaluable. I use a massive e-mail list at my nonprofit, Special Needs Network, to populate events, educate constituents about key policy issues, and raise millions of dollars for autism.

Being a rainmaker will absolutely cause money to flow to your bottom line. I can attest to the fact that it brings in new business like nothing else.

Doing Well to Do Good

While monetization is essential, my own motivation for media appearances is more than financial. In fact, for me, being in the media gives me an opportunity to speak out on issues that I care deeply about, such as autism, children, social justice, civil and women's rights, and underserved communities.

As I am the mother of a son on the autism spectrum, Special Needs Network is dear to my heart. The board, members, and supporters of the organization have built a community that nourishes my spirit every day. My media presence is a huge asset to my philanthropy. It helps me raise millions of dollars and attract huge numbers of donors and sponsors for kids with special needs.

In October 2015 we held our tenth annual Evening Under the Stars: The Future is Bright gala. It was a red carpet fund-raiser, attended by celebrities such as Angela Bassett, Kathy Bates, Kym Whitley, and Sheila E on the Sony Studios lot. Five hundred guests were treated to a delicious meal catered by Wolfgang Puck's famed caterers, and Grammy-nominated artists B. Slade and Angie Fisher gave a live performance. The generosity of donors made this magical night possible. If we had had to pay for the appearances of these performing artists and celebrities, we could never have been able to afford it.

There is no doubt that being a rainmaker will have a direct impact on your bottom line, but it can also give you a lot more leverage to help the people you care about most.

As Samantha Schacher says, "The journey is definitely full of peaks and valleys, plenty of roadblocks, and many, many detours. You'll hear the word 'No'—a lot!—but don't let that deter you. You only need one 'Yes' to get the ball rolling."

It took me a long time to learn how to leverage my Harvard law degree and decades of legal practice in these media-intense and digitally focused times. I'm now sharing with you how I did the work to build my followers and brand to have the kind of platform that makes high-profile fund-raisers like these happen. You can do the same thing. It won't happen overnight, but the result will be a more vibrant business and a richer, more dynamic life.

Remember that a rainmaker is an expert with a media presence, who leverages that visibility to build revenue, followers, and influence. If you're reading this, the chances are good that you're already an expert or well on your way to becoming one. You've heard my stories about life in the media and learned the steps you need to take to create a media presence that you can use to completely revolutionize your business and your brand.

Now it's time for you to put everything you've learned into practice. Then step back and watch it rain!

Acknowledgments

If you are fortunate in life, you will have, in addition to your close relatives, a couple of very special people in your life—individuals who love you unconditionally and who support you no matter what the circumstances. I have been blessed to have in my life more than my fair share of such people. Without them, this book would not have been possible.

To my amazing family—Ernest, Michael, Morgan, and Marty—words can hardly express my gratitude to you. Your supportive spirit encouraged me during the toughest days of this journey—days when I simply needed more than twenty-four hours to accomplish everything on my to-do list. Thank you for pitching in, doing the grocery shopping, and even planning the family holiday dinners as I worked to meet the various deadlines set by my publishers. You are the wind beneath my wings, and I couldn't be more proud to be your wife and mother.

And although they have passed on, every year my love and respect for my mother, Doris, my grandmother Doveanne, and my godmother Ethel grow exponentially. Every time I share my story of growing up in St. Louis, I am reminded of the giant shoulders I stand on and the profound impact each of you had on my life. Your collective strength and resilience are legendary. Without your example, I cannot begin to imagine what my life would be like. I know that each of you are forever watching over and guiding me with your loving spirits, and for that I am eternally grateful. I will always be your "Rebie."

To my father, Ronaldo Sr., whom I lost in 2017, thank you for always telling me I was smart. I know fathers are supposed to say nice things to their kids, but your positive affirmation inspired me to work harder and do more.

To my great, big, blended family: stepmom, Kathleen; stepdad, Leon; play mom, Luvenia; brothers Eric, Rodney, Tory, Tony, Howard, and Paul; sister, Rhyanne; stepsisters Ericka, Sarah, and Kimberly; stepbrothers Donnell, JaJa, Adam, and Lee, Jr., thank you for loving and supporting me.

To the matriarch of the family, my dear aunt Lois, you inspire me each and every day with your positive attitude and fearless commitment to live out loud. Thank you for teaching me that my attitude, not my circumstances, determines my destiny.

To my beautiful aunts Alberta, Gwen, Barbara, Iris, and Robbie, you are all amazing women who have taught me that strong women don't play victim or point fingers; they stand tall and deal.

To my sisters and cousins, Robin, Terri, Lori, Pat, Cheryl, Sherna, Antonia, Ruth, LaShawn, Vivian, Sha'ron, Sharon, and Rosemarie, friendship isn't about whom you've known the longest. It's about who walks into your life and says "You can count on me," and then proves it. Thank you for being those friends.

To the Martin, Neely, Crosby, Goins, and Taylor clans, who have always supported me and my many efforts, thank you for all of the virtual love and keeping my social media feeds filled with expressions of encouragement. The "likes and engagement" matter!

Thank you to my friends and colleagues who participated in interviews and allowed me to tell their stories in the book: Dr. Drew Pinsky, Sam Schacher, Brian Ross Adams, Anahita Sedaghatfar, Eric Guster, Eduardo Lucero, and Timothy Snell. I am certain that your success stories will inspire so many others.

Thanks to my professional team, whose leadership has been invaluable to me from the writing of the book's original proposal almost two years ago and whose brilliance made this project possible. To my collaborator, Donna Beech, thank you for bringing your *"New York Times* Best Seller" expertise to this project. You are talented beyond belief! This is number two for us, and I look forward to many more projects in the future.

A heart-filled thank you to my literary agent, Jill Marsal, whose wisdom and vision made this book possible. It means the world to me that you saw that certain something in the proposal, were relentless in vigorously representing a fellow Harvard Law School graduate, and found this project a home.

Thank you to my editor, Christina Boys, and the Hachette Book Group team. Thank you for believing in me and my vision. Your meticulous editing and insightful suggestions have been invaluable.

A humble thank-you to the great Hilsinger Mendelson public relations team. Without question, Sandi Mendelson, Dave Kass, Deborah Jensen, and Amrit Judge, you are the best publicists in the book game. You take branding, positioning, and amplifying a brand to a new and exciting level!

Bonnie Berry LaMon, you have been with me from the beginning of this journey. I am so fortune to have a Princeton- and Harvard-trained lawyer on my side. It means I get the best of the best in legal representation for each and every project. And as you know, you are so much more than my super lawyer; you are my BFF, ride or die, unofficial manager, counselor, and all-things girlfriend. We are in each other's life for a reason. Thank you for showing up.

A big thank you to Jay McGraw. Jay, you gave me my first TV hosting job on the Emmy Award–winning talk show *The Doctors*. It's been a couple of seasons, and I am having so much fun being the attorney host working with America's top doctors providing millions of viewers with information that they can use to live their best lives! And working with you on not one but two other TV projects has been an absolute blast!

Dr. Phil, plain and simple—*You are the best!* Being a part of the Stage 29 team has not only been a dream come true but the opportunity of a lifetime. Dr. Phil, you gave me my start in the media on the number-one-rated daytime syndicated talk show on television—the *Dr. Phil* show—and you have been one of my biggest supporters for nearly a decade.

Thank you, Dr. Phil, for writing your wonderful foreword to this book and for being such a beloved mentor. I can never thank you enough for believing and investing in me all these years. Your loyalty and friendship mean the world to me. You have taught me so much about how to make transformative TV that empowers people's lives. Let's keep making great TV together!

XoXo

Notes

Chapter 2. Lock On to Your Brand

1. Glenn Llopis. "Personal Branding Is a Leadership Requirement, Not a Self-Promotion Campaign." *Forbes*. Apr. 8, 2013. https://www.forbes.com/sites/glennllopis/2013/04/08/personal-branding-is-a-leadership-requirement-not-a-self-promotion-campaign/#94a71a3226fa.
2. Ibid.
3. Ibid.
4. Dorie Clark. "Reinventing Your Personal Brand." *Harvard Business Review*. Mar. 2011. https://hbr.org/2011/03/reinventing-your-personal-brand.
5. Kirsty Walker. "The Rise and Rise of the Female TV Expert." *Telegraph*. Mar. 22, 2013. http://www.telegraph.co.uk/women/womens-life/9947737/The-rise-and-rise-of-the-female-TV-expert.html.
6. Clark. "Reinventing Your Personal Brand."
7. Ibid.
8. Ibid.
9. Carole Cadwalladr. "Patricia Cornwell: 'I grew up with fear.'" *Guardian*. Nov. 1, 2015. https://www.theguardian.com/books/2015/nov/01/patricia-cornwell-i-grew-up-with-fear#img-1.
10. "Inside Patricia's Life." Patricia Cornwell. http://www.patriciacornwell.com/about/.
11. Clark. "Reinventing Your Personal Brand."

Chapter 3. Find Your People

1. Heather Long. "The New Normal: 4 Job Changes by the Time You're 32." CNN Money. Apr. 12, 2016. http://money.cnn.com/2016/04/12/news/economy/millennials-change-jobs-frequently/.
2. Ben Sailer. "How to Find Your Target Audience and Create the Best Content That Connects." *CoSchedule Blog*. Aug. 1, 2016. https://coschedule.com/blog/how-to-find-your-target-audience/.

3. Ibid.
4. Michael Hyatt. "Please Take My 2013 Reader Survey." Michael Hyatt .com. https://michaelhyatt.com/2013-reader-survey.html.
5. Sailer. "How To Find Your Target Audience."
6. Jim Sterne. *Social Media Metrics: How to Measure and Optimize Your Marketing Investment* (New Rules Social Media Series). Wiley, p. 51.
7. "History of Mother's." Mother's Restaurant. http://www.mothersrest aurant.net/history_facts.html.
8. "Developmental Disabilities." Centers for Disease Control and Prevention. https://www.cdc.gov/ncbddd/developmentaldisabilities/about.html.
9. Sterne. *Social Media Metrics.*
10. Kristen Matthews. "The Definitive Guide to Influencer Targeting." Kissmetrics. https://blog.kissmetrics.com/guide-to-influencer-targeting/.
11. Matthews. "The Definitive Guide."
12. A. J. Agrawal. "Why Influencer Marketing Will Explode in 2017." *Forbes.* Dec. 27, 2016. https://www.forbes.com/sites/ajagrawal/2016/12/27 /why-influencer-marketing-will-explode-in-2017/#50adc9d520a9.
13. Kyle Wong. "The Explosive Growth of Influencer Marketing and What It Means for You." *Forbes.* Sept. 10, 2014. https://www.forbes.com /sites/kylewong/2014/09/10/the-explosive-growth-of-influencer -marketing-and-what-it-means-for-you/2/#14f53dd666c1.
14. James Lane. "What is Klout and What Does My Klout Score Mean?" Hypestar. Feb. 5, 2017. https://www.hypestar.uk/what-is-klout-score-how -raise-klout-score/.
15. Wong. "The Explosive Growth."
16. Matthews. "The Definitive Guide."
17. Sterne. *Social Media Metrics.*
18. Matthews. "The Definitive Guide."
19. Ibid.
20. Agrawal. "Influencer Marketing."
21. Ibid.

Chapter 4. Hone Your Pitch

1. Kelly McCarthy. "Former Bachelorette Kaitlyn Bristowe Opens Up About Decision to Freeze Her Eggs." *Good Morning America.* ABC News. Mar. 22, 2017. http://abcnews.go.com/Entertainment/bachelorette -kaitlyn-bristowe-opens-decision-freeze-eggs/story?id=46292389.

2. "Coast Guard, TSA Could Face Deep Budget Cuts." *Anderson Cooper 360°*. CNN Politics. Mar. 3, 2017. http://edition.cnn.com/videos /politics/2017/03/08/tsa-coast-guard-trump-immigration-budget-marsh -dnt-ac.cnn.

3. Yohana Desta. "Watch a Tearful Adele Use Her Big Grammys Win to Bow Down to Beyoncé." *Vanity Fair*. Feb. 13, 2017. http://www.vanity fair.com/hollywood/2017/02/adele-beyonce-album-of-the-year.

4. Rachel Maddow. *The Rachel Maddow Show*. Transcript. MSNBC. Dec. 19, 2016. http://www.msnbc.com/transcripts/rachel-maddow-show /2016-12-19.

5. "YouTube Top 100 Most Subscribed News & Politics Channels List—Top by Subscribers." VidStatsX.com. https://vidstatsx.com /youtube-top-100-most-subscribed-news-politics-channels.

Chapter 5. Become a Trusted Source

1. Meredith B. Kile. "Exclusive: 'Moonlight' Director Barry Jenkins Reacts to Best Picture Mix-Up: 'It Couldn't Have Been Easy.'" ETOnline .com. Feb. 26, 2017. http://www.etonline.com/awards/oscars/211538 _moonlight_director_barry_jenkins_reacts_to_best_picture_mix_up _it_couldn_t_have_been_easy/.

2. Fox News. "Tucker vs. Bill Nye the Science Guy." YouTube. Feb. 27, 2017. https://www.youtube.com/watch?v=qN5L2q6hfWo.

3. CNN. "CNN'S Exclusive Obama Interview." YouTube. Jan. 31, 2014. https://www.youtube.com/watch?v=WBgwuFM92i4.

4. David Packman Show. "CNN Host Abruptly Ends Show When Panelist Calls It ' "Fake News.' " YouTube. Feb. 23, 2017. https://www.youtube .com/watch?v=OP3UW-s3p2I&t=157s.

Chapter 6. Go for Media Channels—Big and Small

1. "2015–16 Los Angeles County Budget." Los Angeles County Annual Report. http://lacountyannualreport.com/budget/.

2. "Regions and Cities of LA County." Los Angeles County Economic Development Corporation. http://laedc.org/wtc/chooselacounty/regions -of-la-county/.

3. "GDP of the Los Angeles Metro Area from 2001 to 2015 (in Billion U.S. Dollars)." Statista. https://www.statista.com/statistics/183822 /gdp-of-the-los-angeles-metro-area/.

4. "Our Story." Martin Luther King, Jr. Community Hospital. http:// www.mlkcommunityhospital.org/About-Us/Our-Story.aspx.

5. Steve Baron. "List of How Many Homes Each Cable Network Is in as of February 2015." TV by the Numbers. Zap2it. Feb. 22, 2015. http:// tvbythenumbers.zap2it.com/reference/list-of-how-many-homes-each -cable-network-is-in-as-of-february-2015/366230/.

6. "CNN Is First to Stream 24-Hour News Network Online and On Mobile." CNN Press Room. July 18, 2011. http://cnnpressroom.blogs .cnn.com/2011/07/18/cnn-is-first-to-stream-24-hour-news-network -online-and-on-mobile/.

7. Sarah Perez. "ABC News Teams Up with Facebook to Live Stream the 2016 General Election Debates." TechCrunch. Sept. 20, 2016. https://techcrunch.com/2016/09/20/abc-news-teams-up-with -facebook-to-live-stream-the-2016-general-election-debates/.

8. Perez. "ABC News Teams Up."

9. Steven Perlberg and Deepa Seetharaman. "Facebook Signs Deals With Media Companies, Celebrities for Facebook Live." *Wall Street Journal*. June 22, 2016. https://www.wsj.com/articles/facebook-signs-deals -with-media-companies-celebrities-for-facebook-live-1466533472.

10. Ibid.

11. Ibid.

12. Ibid.

13. Erik Sherman. "9 Great Business Podcasts You Should Know." *Fortune*. Dec. 4, 2014. http://fortune.com/2014/12/04/great-business -podcasts/.

14. Sam McRoberts. "10 Podcasts Every Entrepreneur Must Listen To in 2016." *Inc*. Feb. 1, 2016. http://www.inc.com/sam-mcroberts/10-podcasts-every -entrepreneur-must-listen-to-in-2016.html.

15. "Stations for Network—NBC." RabbitEars. http://www.rabbitears .info/search.php?request=network_search&network=NBC.

16. "Stations for Network: CBS." RabbitEars. http://www.rabbitears.info /search.php?request=network_search&network=CBS.

17. Lindsay Lorenz. "WJAR-TV NBC 10 Garners Highest February Viewer- ship." PBN. Mar. 20, 2013. http://www.pbn.com/WJAR-TV-NBC-10 -garners-highest-February-viewership,87212.

18. "WJAR." Revolvy. https://www.revolvy.com/main/index.php?s=W JAR.

19. Douglas Blanks Hindman and Kenneth Wiegand. "The Big Three's Prime-Time Decline: A Technological and Social Context." *Journal of*

Broadcasting & Electronic Media 52(1), 2008, pp. 119–135. Available at https://robertoigarza.files.wordpress.com/2008/10/art-the-big-threes -prime-time-decline-hindman-2008.pdf.

Chapter 7. Jump on Breaking News Stories

1. Garrett Therolf, Frank Shyong, and Rosanna Xia. "Calabasas Fire Is 80% Contained." *Los Angeles Times.* June 5, 2016. http://www.latimes .com/local/lanow/la-me-ln-temecula-fire-20160604-snap-story.html.
2. Ibid.
3. Benjamin Mullin. "Mashable Says It's Thriving by Embracing Quality Journalism—and Avoiding the Same Old Trump Stories." Poynter. Feb. 22, 2017. https://www.poynter.org/2017/mashable-says-its-thriving -by-embracing-quality-journalism-and-focus-and-avoiding-the-same -old-trump-stories/449560/.
4. Ibid.
5. Ibid.
6. Kit Smith. "Marketing: Amazing Social Media Statistics and Facts." Brandwatch. Mar. 7, 2016. https://www.brandwatch.com/2016/03/96 -amazing-social-media-statistics-and-facts-for-2016/.
7. "As Mobile Grows Rapidly, Pressures on News Intensify." State of the Media. http://www.stateofthemedia.org/2013/digital-as-mobile-grows -rapidly-the-pressures-on-news-intensify/digital-by-the-numbers/.
8. Katerina Eva Matsa and Kristine Lu. "10 Facts About the Changing Digital News Landscape." Pew Research Center. Sept. 14, 2016. http://www.pewresearch.org/fact-tank/2016/09/14/facts-about-the -changing-digital-news-landscape/.
9. "Level of Interest in Various News Types in the U.S. in 2015." Statista. https://www.statista.com/statistics/254511/level-of-interest -in-various-news-types-in-the-us/.
10. *State of the News Media 2016.* Pew Research Center. June 15, 2016. http://assets.pewresearch.org/wp-content/uploads/sites/13/2016 /06/30143308/state-of-the-news-media-report-2016-final.pdf.
11. Mark Jurkowitz et al. "The State of the News Media 2013." Pew Research Center. http://www.stateofthemedia.org/2013/special-reports-landing -page/the-changing-tv-news-landscape/.
12. "Number of Newly Developed Applications/Games Submitted for Release to the iTunes App Store from 2012 to 2016." Statista. https:// www.statista.com/statistics/258160/number-of-new-apps-submitted -to-the-itunes-store-per-month/.

13. "January 2017 Ratings—MSNBC Racks Up Higher Total Viewer Growth Than CNN and Fox News Across Key Dayparts." MSNBC. Jan. 31, 2017. http://info.msnbc.com/_news/2017/01/31/36810479 -january-2017-ratings-msnbc-racks-up-higher-total-viewer-growth -than-cnn-and-fox-news-across-key-dayparts.

14. Marisa Guthrie. "Rachel Maddow: How This Wonky-Tonk Woman Won TV." *Hollywood Reporter.* Oct. 5, 2011. http://www.hollywoodre porter.com/news/rachel-maddow-msnbc-243775.

15. "Rachel Maddow Biography." The Famous People. http://www.thefa mouspeople.com/profiles/rachel-maddow-4074.php.

16. Guthrie. "Rachel Maddow: How This Wonky-Tonk Woman Won TV."

17. Ibid.

Chapter 8. Forget the Old Social Media

1. Larry Kim. "15 Mind-Blowing Statistics Reveal What Happens on the Internet in a Minute [Infographic]." *Inc.* Oct. 27, 2015. http:// www.inc.com/larry-kim/15-mind-blowing-statistics-reveal-what -happens-on-the-internet-in-a-minute.html.

2. "The Top 20 Valuable Facebook Statistics." Zephoria. Feb. 21, 2017. https://zephoria.com/top-15-valuable-facebook-statistics/.

3. "Number of Monthly Active Twitter Users Worldwide from 1st Quarter 2010 to 4h Quarter 2016." Statista. https://www.statista.com /statistics/282087/number-of-monthly-active-twitter-users/.

4. "YouTube Company Statistics." Statistic Brain Research Institute. Sept. 1, 2016. http://www.statisticbrain.com/youtube-statistics/. "36 Mind-Blowing YouTube Facts, Figures and Statistics—2017." Fortunelords. https://fortunelords.com/youtube-statistics/.

5. "Statistics." YouTube. https://www.youtube.com/yt/press/statistics.html.

6. Eric Markowitz. "How Instagram Grew from Foursquare Knock-off to $1 Billion Photo Empire." *Inc.* Apr. 10, 2012. http://www.inc.com/eric -markowitz/life-and-times-of-instagram-the-complete-original-story .html.

7. Ibid.

8. Ibid.

9. Ibid.

10. Ibid.

11. "Number of Monthly Active Instgram Users from January 2013 to December 2016." Statista. https://www.statista.com/statistics/253577 /number-of-monthly-active-instagram-users/.

12. Michelle Castillo. "Snapchat Is King Among Teens as Facebook Declines in Popularity." CNBC. Oct. 13, 2016. http://www.cnbc.com/2016 /10/13/snapchat-is-king-among-teens-as-facebook-declines -in-popularity-survey-shows.html.

13. James Titcomb and Sam Dean. "Snapchat IPO: $24bn app Jumps as Much as 40pc in Blockbuster Tech Float—and Makes 26-year-old Founder Evan Spiegel Worth $5bn." *Telegraph*. Mar. 2, 2017. http:// www.telegraph.co.uk/technology/2017/03/02/snapchat-ipo-snap -worth-24bn-blockbuster-tech-float-live/.

14. Shira Ovide and Rani Molla. "Five Charts Explaining Why Snapchat's Worth $25 Billion." Bloomberg. Oct. 7, 2016. https://www.bloomberg .com/gadfly/articles/2016-10-07/snapchat-ipo-5-charts-explaining -why-it-s-worth-25-billion.

15. JD Gershbein. "The LinkedIn Groups Have Become Ghost Towns." *Huffington Post*. Mar 22, 2016. http://www.huffingtonpost.com/jd-gershbein /linkedin-groups-have-become-ghost-towns_b_9509092.html.

16. Llopis. "Personal Branding" (see chap. 2, n. 1).

17. Vinny La Barbera. "6 Online Marketing Strategy Questions You MUST Answer." imFORZA. https://www.imforza.com/blog/online -marketing-strategy-questions-you-must-answer/.

18. "About Us." GoPro. https://gopro.com/about-us.

19. "Shonda Rhimes Teaches Writing for Television." MasterClass. https:// www.masterclass.com/classes/shonda-rhimes-teaches-writing-for -television?utm_source=Paid&utm_medium=AdWords&utm_ter m=Aq-Prospecting&utm_content=Search&utm_campaign=SR.

20. David Silverstein, Phil Samuel, and Neil DeCarlo. "Technique 1: Jobs to Be Done." *The Innovator's Toolkit*. http://innovatorstoolkit.com /content/technique-1-jobs-be-done.

21. Anne Trafton. "In the Blink of an Eye." MIT News. Jan. 16, 2014. http://news.mit.edu/2014/in-the-blink-of-an-eye-0116.

22. Larry Kim. "16 Eye-Popping Statistics You Need to Know About Visual Content Marketing." *Inc*. Nov. 23, 2015. http://www.inc.com /larry-kim/visual-content-marketing-16-eye-popping-statistics-you -need-to-know.html.

23. "Photos Cluttering Your Facebook Feed? Here's Why." Apr. 21, 2014. eMarketer. https://www.emarketer.com/Article/Photos-Cluttering -Your-Facebook-Feed-Herersquos-Why/1010777.

24. Belle Beth Cooper. "How Twitter's Expanded Images Increase Clicks, Retweets and Favorites [New Data]." Buffer. Apr. 27, 2016. https://

blog.bufferapp.com/the-power-of-twitters-new-expanded-images
-and-how-to-make-the-most-of-it.

25. Kim. "16 Eye-Popping Statistics."

26. Mark Hyman, MD. @drmarkhyman. Facebook. June 18, 2017, 3:00 p.m. https://www.facebook.com/drmarkhyman/.

27. Ibid. June 16, 2017, 3:00 p.m.

28. Ibid. Aug. 1, 2017, 1:22 a.m.

29. Glenn Leibowitz. "10 Social Media Strategies Successful Authors Use to Sell More Books." *Inc.* Apr. 12, 2016. http://www.inc.com/glenn -leibowitz/10-social-media-strategies-successful-authors-use-to-sell -more-books.html.

30. Ibid.

Chapter 9. Engage or Fail

1. Thomas Smith. *Successful Advertising: Its Secrets Explained.* 9th ed. (London: Smith's Advertising Agency, 1899).

2. Herbert E. Krugman. "The Impact of Television Advertising: Learning Without Involvement." *Public Opinion Quarterly* 29(3), Autumn 1965, pp. 349–356. https://www.jstor.org/stable/2746936?seq=1#page_scan _tab_contents.

3. Molly Freudenberg. "The Facebook Fix: 7 Proven Strategies to Get Your Posts Seen on Facebook." CreativeLIVE Blog. May 3, 2016. http:// blog.creativelive.com/facebook-marketing-strategy/.

4. Alex Chris. "How to Get Your First 10,000 Fans on Facebook (Case Study)." Reliablesoft.net. Mar. 13, 2017. https://www.reliablesoft.net /how-to-get-your-first-10000-fans-on-facebook-case-study/.

5. Andrew Hutchison. "Do Page Likes Still Matter on Facebook?" Social-MediaToday. July 27, 2016. http://www.socialmediatoday.com/social -networks/do-page-likes-still-matter-facebook.

6. Ibid.

7. Freudenberg. "The Facebook Fix."

8. Vinny La Barbera. "Growing a Social Following from Scratch." imFORZA. https://www.imforza.com/blog/growing-a-social-following -from-scratch/.

9. Ibid.

10. Chris Campbell. "3 Things Every Marketer Should Know about Reviews and Ratings on Facebook." SocialMediaToday. July 26, 2016. http://www.socialmediatoday.com/social-networks/3-things-every -marketer-should-know-about-reviews-and-ratings-facebook.

11. Hutchison. "Do Page Likes Still Matter on Facebook?"
12. Campbell. "3 Things."
13. Neil Patel. "How Frequently You Should Post on Social Media According to the Pros." *Forbes*. Sept 12, 2016. https://www.forbes.com/sites/neilpatel/2016/09/12/how-frequently-you-should-post-on-social-media-according-to-the-pros/.
14. Freudenberg. "The Facebook Fix."
15. Kevan Lee. "How Often to Post to Facebook, Twitter, LinkedIn and More." Buffer. Aug 29, 2016. https://stories.buffer.com/how-often-to-post-to-facebook-twitter-linkedin-and-more-bb2758459162#.827aczj3x.
16. Patel. "How Frequently You Should Post."
17. Ibid.
18. Lee. "How Often to Post."
19. Ibid.
20. Freudenberg. "The Facebook Fix."
21. Sam Street. "All's Wel That Ends Wel: Danny Welbeck Does Salt Bae Celebration After Scoring Two Goals on His Arsenal Return from 265 Days out Injured." *Sun*. Jan. 29, 2017. https://www.thesun.co.uk/sport/football/2729620/danny-welbeck-does-the-salt-bae-celebration-after-scoring-two-goals-on-his-arsenal-return-from-265-days-out-injured/.
22. Jay Hathaway. "The Absolute Best Memes of 2017 (Thus Far)." *Daily Dot*. Feb 1, 2017. https://www.dailydot.com/unclick/best-memes-2017/.
23. Josie Griffiths. "Who Is Salt Bae aka Nusret Gökçe, Where Is He Opening a London Steakhouse and Why Did the Turkish Chef Season Leonardo DiCaprio's Steak?" *Sun*. Feb. 3, 2017. https://www.thesun.co.uk/living/2709075/salt-bae-nusret-gokce-london-steakhouse-leonardo-di-caprio/.
24. Elijah Watson. "The Photographer Who Gave Us Crying Jordan Had No Idea It Was a Meme." *Daily Dot*. May 23, 2016. https://www.dailydot.com/unclick/crying-jordan-meme-photographer/.
25. Hathaway. "The Absolute Best Memes of 2017."
26. *The Color Purple* on Broadway. "A Tribute to Prince from the Cast of *The Color Purple*." YouTube. Apr. 21, 2016. https://www.youtube.com/watch?v=W6KUTL0PXl0.
27. *The Late Late Show with James Corden*. "First Lady Michelle Obama Carpool Karaoke." YouTube. July 20, 2016. https://www.youtube.com/watch?v=ln3wAdRAim4.

Chapter 10. Wield Your Connections

1. Keith Ferrazzi and Tahl Raz. *Never Eat Alone: And Other Secrets to Success, One Relationship at a Time*. New York: Crown Business, 2014, Kindle location 358.

2. Ibid.

3. Elizabeth Joh. "Free Police Body Cameras Come with a Price." *Future Tense* (blog). *Slate*. Apr. 5, 2017. http://www.slate.com/blogs/future_tense/2017/04/05/taser_international_now_axon_offers_police_free_body_cameras.html.

4. Ferrazzi. *Never Eat Alone*.

5. Ibid.

6. Ibid.

7. Ibid.

8. Mike Masnick. "How Neil Gaiman Went from Fearing 'Piracy' to Believing It's 'an Incredibly Good Thing.'" Techdirt. Feb. 11, 2011. https://www.techdirt.com/articles/20110211/00384413053/how-neil-gaiman-went-fearing-piracy-to-believing-its-incredibly-good-thing.shtml.

9. Ibid.

10. Ibid.

11. Angela Ponsford. "Facebook Ads Case Study: How an Advertising 'FAIL' Can Actually Turn into a 'WIN.'" Claire Pelletreau. Dec. 10, 2015. http://clairepells.com/facebook-ads-case-study-fail-to-win/.

12. "Hello—I'm Amelia Lee, the Undercover Architect." Undercover Architect. http://undercoverarchitect.com/about-amelia-lee-undercover-architect/.

13. Ferrazzi. *Never Eat Alone*.

Chapter 11. Watch It Rain

1. Luke Graham. "Are Podcasts Missing Out on a Huge—and Lucrative—Audience?" CNBC. Aug. 24, 2016. http://www.cnbc.com/2016/08/24/are-podcasts-missing-out-on-a-huge—and-lucrative—audience.html.

2. Gabriela Taylor. *Socialize to Monetize: How to Run Effective Social Media Campaigns Across the Top 25 Social Networking Sites* (Give Your Marketing a Digital Edge Series). CreateSpace Independent Publishing Platform, 2012, p. 1.

3. "Los Angeles Times Display Advertising Rates." Nationwide Newspapers Advertising. http://www.nationwideadvertising.com/sanfrch1coin.html.

4. Michael Wolf. "Ever Wonder How Many Downloads the Big Podcasts Get? Here Are Some Answers." NextMarket. May 16, 2013. http://blog.nextmarket.co/post/50600921448/ever-wonder-how-many-downloads-the-big-podcasts.

5. Rebecca Greenfield. "The (Surprisingly Profitable) Rise of Podcast Networks." Fast Company. Sept. 26, 2014. https://www.fastcompany.com/3035954/the-surprisingly-profitable-rise-of-podcast-networks.

6. Katerina Eva Matsa. "Local TV News: Fact Sheet." In *State of the News Media 2016* (see chap. 7, n. 10).

7. Andrew Perrin. "One-Fifth of Americans Report Going Online 'Almost Constantly.'" Fact Tank. Pew Research Center. Dec. 8, 2015. http://www.pewresearch.org/fact-tank/2015/12/08/one-fifth-of-americans-report-going-online-almost-constantly/.

8. "Who's Reading Newspapers These Days." Media Life. Dec. 16, 2015. http://www.medialifemagazine.com/whos-reading-newspapers-days/.

9. Gaby Dunn. "Get Rich or Die Vlogging: The Sad Economics of Internet Fame." Splinter. Dec. 14, 2015. http://splinternews.com/get-rich-or-die-vlogging-the-sad-economics-of-internet-1793853578.

10. Madeline Berg. "The Highest-Paid YouTube Stars 2016: PewDiePie Remains No. 1 with $15 Million." *Forbes.* Dec. 20, 2016. https://www.forbes.com/sites/maddieberg/2016/12/05/the-highest-paid-youtube-stars-2016-pewdiepie-remains-no-1-with-15-million/#9f9a26977132.

11. Matt Branham. "Meet the Filthy Rich YouTube Stars." Crave. Feb. 3, 2015. http://www.craveonline.com/mandatory/1056846-meet-the-filthy-rich-stars-of-youtube.

12. Mark W. Schaefer. *Return on Influence: The Revolutionary Power of Klout, Social Scoring, and Influence Marketing.* New York: McGraw-Hill Education, Kindle ed., p. 84.

13. Berg. "The Highest-Paid YouTube Stars."

14. Ibid.

15. Ibid.

16. Leibowitz. "10 Social Media Strategies" (see chap. 8, n. 29).

17. Berg. "The Highest-Paid YouTube Stars."

18. Ibid.

19. Dorie Clark. "How to Become a Successful Professional Speaker." *Forbes.* June 10, 2013. https://www.forbes.com/sites/dorieclark/2013/06/10/how-to-become-a-successful-professional-speaker/.

20. Ibid.

21. Tom Antion. "Top Ten Ways to Make Money Public Speaking." Advanced Public Speaking Institute. http://www.public-speaking.org/topten.htm.

22. Clark. "How to Become a Successful Professional Speaker."

23. Lauren Smith. "Email Preferred Communication Channel; Commands More Clicks & ROI." Litmus. Feb. 20, 2013. https://litmus.com/blog/email-preferred-more-clicks-conversions-roi.

24. Vinny La Barbera. "Building an Email List from Scratch." imFORZA. https://www.imforza.com/blog/building-an-email-list-from-scratch/.

25. Kevan Lee. "Email List-Building from the Experts: How to Grow a Massive Email List." Buffer. Feb. 1, 2016. https://blog.bufferapp.com/email-list-building.

26. La Barbera. "Building an Email List from Scratch."

27. Ibid.

28. Ibid.

Index

About the Authors

Areva Martin

Known to audiences across the country, Areva Martin is an attorney, an advocate, a television host, a legal and social issues commentator, and an author. She is one of television's most in-demand legal experts/analysts. A recurring cohost on the Emmy Award—winning syndicated talk show *The Doctors* and a CNN legal analyst, Areva appears regularly on *Dr. Phil*, *Anderson Cooper 360°*, *Good Morning America*, *World News Tonight*, *Smercornish*, *CNN International*, *CNN Tonight*, and a variety of talk and news shows.

A quotable authority on workplace, disability rights, education, custody, and women's issues, this accomplished and multi-award-winning attorney, syndicated columnist, and public speaker is also quoted and/or featured on the pages of publications ranging from *Redbook* to the *Huffington Post*. Areva writes regularly for CNN.com, the *Daily Beast*, and *Time—Motto*.

Areva, a Harvard-trained civil rights attorney, is the founding and managing partner of one of Los Angeles's oldest and largest African-American female-owned law firms, Martin & Martin, LLP. She has been identified as a Southern California Super Lawyer for the last five years. She is also the founder and president of Special Needs Network, California's premier autism advocacy organization.

The mother of three, Areva is an avid runner who lives in Los Angeles with her family.

Donna Beech

Donna Beech is a *New York Times* best-selling and award-winning coauthor who has worked on dozens of books, including *New York Times* best seller *Ghost in the Wires*, *The Everyday Advocate*, *Total Recovery*, and *The HeartMath Solution*.